*They were ready to use
their painful weapons.*

Crawling across the floor were two huge scorpions. They slid along together, tails curled overhead, ready to use their painful weapons.

Her right hand flew to her mouth, stifling the scream that lodged behind her clenched teeth.

The scream escaped and shredded the night air as she spotted the third scorpion, poised three inches from her left hand, in the bed with her.

THE MUMMY

BARBARA STEINER

SCHOLASTIC INC.
New York Toronto London Auckland Sydney

No part of this publication may be reproduced in whole or in part, or stored in a retrieval system, or transmitted in any form or by any means, electronic, mechanical, photocopying, recording, or otherwise, without written permission of the publisher. For information regarding permission, write to Scholastic Inc., 555 Broadway, New York, NY 10012.

ISBN 0-590-20353-3

12 11 10 9 8 7 6 5 4 3 2 1   5 6 7 8 9/9 0/0

Printed in the U.S.A.   01

First Scholastic printing, May 1995

For Jimmy and Ruth Marie Lyons,
Egypt fans and good friends.

Chapter 1

"This coffin is empty," Dr. David Walters said, pointing to an ornately painted wooden coffin, "because someone robbed the grave of the princess Urbena and took her mummy." He smiled, tilted his head slightly, and looked at the group gathered around him, especially the reporters. "Legend tells us there is a curse on the tomb that will be broken only when the mummy of Urbena is found and returned."

Was it Lana's imagination or did Dr. Walters' eyes stop at hers for a split second and did he wink?

"Do you believe in the curse?" a reporter from the *Denver Post* asked.

"Common sense says no, but everyone who was on the expedition when they dug up Urbena's sarcophagus has died."

Lana shivered. Was that really true?

Marge Wilson, a retired teacher who was a

long-time volunteer at the Denver Museum, stood beside Lana. She whispered, "Notice he didn't say *how* they died. Those relics from her tomb were discovered in 1937. Old age would have set in by now."

Lana giggled and felt better, even though common sense told her that believing in curses was pure superstition. But then, every decent tomb had to have a curse on it or what fun were they?

"The press loves the idea," Lana whispered back. "They'll make sure people come and see the exhibit." She and Marge followed the small crowd around Dr. Walters back into the main exhibit hall.

The news conference broke up then, and Lana saw someone across the room beside the refreshment table whom she wanted to meet. "Excuse me, Marge."

"Miss Vaughn?" Lana stopped a tall, athletic-looking woman. She had long reddish-blonde hair that Lana thought was beautiful. Tonight Blair Vaughn had caught it up in an ornate barrette that could only have come from Egypt. The young woman stopped and stared at Lana as if she was surprised that someone had spoken to her.

"Yes?" There was no smile on Blair Vaughn's face that encouraged Lana to continue, but Lana went on, wondering why Blair Vaughn was unfriendly.

"I'm Alana Richardson. People call me Lana. I've wanted to meet you ever since I heard you were coming. You're quite a well-known archaeologist for someone so young."

The woman's face softened a little at the compliment. She set her punch cup on the table and reached for Lana's hand to shake it. "People don't usually recognize me."

Lana took Blair's cold hand in a firm grip. "Dr. Walters pointed you out to me after the Egypt Society meeting. He said I should talk to you if I was at all interested in archaeology as a career."

"And are you?" Blair withdrew her hand and stared at Lana. She was certainly direct and not a babbler. Sometimes when Lana got excited words spilled out until she was embarrassed by talking so much. She was trying not to do that now, trying to act as cool and sophisticated as Blair.

"I think so. But I wouldn't want to work just any place. I've been totally interested in Egypt since sixth grade."

"You look Egyptian, you know. I'm rather envious of that long, black hair." Blair reached out and touched Lana's shoulder-length hair.

Lana was speechless, not usually one of her

problems. But she knew she looked Egyptian. She had gone to a styling salon with a picture of an Egyptian queen in her hand. "Cut my hair to look like this," she'd said. The hairdresser loved the idea, and Lana's hair, thick and jet-black, held the blunt cut perfectly.

With the remark about Lana's look, Blair Vaughn became almost friendly. "Actually, now I remember that Dr. Walters said he had a student he wanted me to meet. He said you read and write hieroglyphics and have a good knowledge of Egyptian mythology as well as the history."

"He's being kind. I've only started with my study." Lana found her voice. She did know a lot about Egypt, but there was so much to learn.

"I think you're being modest. You can't do that, you know. You really have to be aggressive in this field today. Men are still given the best digs, and they become known faster."

"Even when *you* know as much as they do?" Lana knew Blair Vaughn was one of the top experts in the field of Egyptology right now. She was working at a site in Egypt, or had been. She had taken time off to come to Denver with this special exhibit.

"That's right." Blair smiled. "Excuse me, Lana. I want to talk to Dr. Walters before he leaves." Blair walked quickly across the room. She had so much poise, Lana was a bit in awe of the woman. She felt good that Blair had finally warmed up enough to talk to her. Maybe they'd get a chance to talk while the show was in Denver. Lana would like to get as many ideas and as much advice as possible from the successsful archaeologist.

The Denver Museum of Natural History was fortunate to get the Egyptian exhibit. This was the last stop before returning to Cairo. It took all the control Lana had not to jump up and down with excitement just to be surrounded by all these treasures.

She stood alone, listening to stray comments — excited voices — of those at the party who were also enthusiastic about the show. She wished she could have talked Josh into coming with her tonight. This opening was only for museum staff and volunteers like herself, who'd worked on the exhibit, but they could each bring a guest.

Josh Benson was as plainspoken as Blair. He'd said he didn't want to come look at "that musty old stuff." Sometimes Lana got frustrated because she and Josh had so little in common — except liking each other. Well, they had school and school activities, but not much else.

She sighed and decided to look at the "musty old stuff" one more time herself before the evening was over. Not that she hadn't seen them. She smiled. She couldn't get enough of seeing them. But leading groups through the show wasn't going to be the same as being alone with the artifacts.

Heading back to the second room of the exhibit, she glanced quickly at a gold pendant in the form of a lapis-lazuli scarab beetle; an alabaster vase, decorated with inlaid lapis; and a silver cup worked with a riot of grapevines along the lip. Some of the statues of animals, especially cats, which the Egyptians worshiped, fascinated her. She had read that one excavation revealed the mummies of three hundred thousand cats. Plus some mummified mice so the cats wouldn't be hungry on their journey to the other side. She smiled at that idea.

All the time she stared into the cases, however, she tried to ignore the strange feeling that had come over her again. She had had it before. It was a magnetic, almost hypnotic, pull to one section of this back room . . . to the mummies.

It was the mummies that held the most fascination for her. The mummies who seemed to call to her now. She glanced around quickly.

No one she knew was near her. She hadn't told anyone about this strange feeling she had had. Blair Vaughn would probably laugh at her. Marge might not laugh, but she'd surely tease Lana. Lana didn't know whether to laugh herself, or be frightened.

She walked slowly toward the coffins, then paused, making sure she could turn away, making it clear that she was in charge of her feelings. Was she? She ran her hand over an ornately decorated coffin, Urbena's coffin.

Death was an incredibly complex ritual for ancient Egyptian people — not just for the kings and queens, but anyone who could afford an expensive funeral. Spending a fortune burying a relative was a sign of how much you respected them.

She stopped and stared at another mummy of a cat. It was hard to believe that some of the sacred cats had been prepared and buried with the gauze wrapping and same ceremony as the pharaohs. She didn't know why, but it bothered her more to think of a cat being buried this way than it did a person.

Quickly, giving in to her feelings, she moved to the star of this show, Prince Nefra, and his coffin. The face carved on the lid was incredibly handsome. Nefra's huge, dark wooden eyes seemed to stare back at her. Nineteen

— he was only nineteen when he died . . . on the eve of his wedding day. That was what made the story such a tragedy.

No one seemed to know why, but on the night before Nefra was to marry the princess Urbena, he sickened and died. Lana tried to imagine how such an experience would make her feel. Her father had died when she was young. She must have missed him then, but she could scarcely remember him or his death. Those feelings had long disappeared, and she couldn't call them up to re-experience them. Here she was, fascinated by death, Egyptian style, when she herself remembered nothing of the feeling, the actual loss.

She looked at Nefra's mummy again. The gauze had darkened with time to grays and in some places black. Maybe she didn't really believe the body of the young prince was inside all those bandages. If you thought too much about it, this sight was almost too much to absorb. She could see the hollow spaces of his eyes, the high bump that was his nose, the soft mounds of his lips. She could imagine his beautiful smile as he had looked at his bride.

Raising her own eyes, she stared at his face on the coffin. Nefra stared back. Lana was inexplicably drawn to him.

Glancing behind her, Lana realized she was

alone in the room with the actual mummy of Nefra and the empty coffin of Urbena. Everyone else had left. It was too quiet.

The lights flickered, signaling that it was time to close, time for this evening to be over. She took joy in knowing there would be many more. She now even accepted the spell Nefra had cast over her, for she *knew* the magnetic pull came from him. She had thought about him so much, she felt she had been part of his life.

She realized how far her imagination had carried her when she whispered to the young king, "Good-bye, Nefra. I'm leaving for tonight, but I'll come back. You know I will, don't you? I can't stay away." She smiled down at him, half expecting him to smile back.

She caught her breath when the lights flickered for the second time and snapped off. Within seconds Lana was surrounded by a darkness that was as complete as that of a tomb.

She clutched the sides of the wooden coffin, feeling the solidness of it. She waited for the lights to come back on, holding herself rigid, pushing back the first trickle of fear in her chest and stomach.

Taking a deep breath, she could smell the age of the body lying beside her. The musty gauze, underground for thousands of years, gave off a dusty, earthy odor.

She pulled her bottom lip between her teeth and bit down gently to keep from calling out. Surely, any second now . . .

But at that moment the whispering started, echoing all around her.

"Princess Urbena, come. Come to me! You are mine. You must come to me!"

Chapter 2

"Come back, Princess. Come back! You belong to me."

The words echoed in the hollow room, became sibilant air that buzzed in her ears, circled her head, and bounced off the walls. She wanted to scream, to call out for help, but there was no air left in her lungs. She had held her breath until her chest ached, her temples throbbed, and she felt faint. Slowly she drew in the musty air around her.

Forcing a rhythm of air in, air out, air in, air out, she squeezed her eyes shut and bent forward. Until she realized she was leaning over the mummy who had spoken.

The *mummy* had spoken? No way!

As the whispers faded into the dark corners around her, rational thought returned her courage. Surely she had imagined the voice.

Taking several more deep breaths, she

stood still and willed the lights to come back on. But the room was filled only with silence, a silence that stretched back thousands of years. The silence of a tomb. The silence of death.

Stop it! Lana, stop it! She pushed away her thoughts. She must move. She must make her way out of this room and into the rest of the museum where a crowd of people also waited for the lights to come on.

She felt her way around the open coffin and started across empty space, her hands stretched in front of her. She tried to picture the arrangement of the artifacts. Almost immediately she bumped into the coffin of Urbena, side by side with Nefra.

At that moment, the lights returned. She blinked her eyes, trying to adjust to the brightness. The first thing to come into focus was the empty coffin prepared for the princess.

Shivering, she hurried into the next room, also empty. Where was everyone? She ran toward the hall.

"Where've you been, Lana?" Marge asked, stopping her flight. "Do you want a ride home?"

"Oh, please, Marge, if it's not out of your way. I have to admit, when the lights went off and caught me in there alone with those mummies, I got a little spooked." Lana tried to laugh.

"The lights? The lights weren't off out here." Marge's round, chubby face changed from her usual smile to a frown. "You got trapped with the mummies?" She laughed her hardy, no-nonsense laugh. "I don't blame you for getting shivery. I don't like looking at them in the daylight." She took Lana's arm. "Come on, I've had enough talk of death and murder and suicide for one night."

"Murder?" Lana hurried along with Marge. "Who was murdered?"

"Oh, you missed another story. Dr. Walters gave the reporters more sensational gossip to print. Said some think Nefra was murdered and then Princess Urbena committed suicide.

Lana gasped at the idea, but she didn't say anything. It was hard to talk and keep up with Marge at the same time. The woman, despite her bulk, moved out of the museum and across the parking lot at a rapid pace, her sensible, rubber-soled shoes thudding on the pavement. Their feet made the only sound in the dark night, and Lana was glad not to be alone.

In Marge's comfortable old Mercedes, Lana caught her breath and questioned Marge further. "Why did Urbena commit suicide? Because Nefra died? I read that he died of some rare disease."

"A rare disease could have been poison. They didn't have medical examiners who had ways of proving how people died in those days. Urbena would have committed suicide because she believed if she died at the same time, she could reincarnate when Nefra did. They'd get back together that way. Of course, often everyone in a pharaoh's court was killed when he died. The ancient Egyptians were thorough in that way. Probably the next king wanted his own servants so he could trust them. Things aren't too different today, except the president just fires everyone in the old administration." Marge laughed again. Lana liked the older woman because it was hard to stay gloomy or frightened when around her.

Lana thought about Urbena killing herself. Suicide was a pretty drastic step to take. "Do you believe in reincarnation, Marge?"

"I don't know. Sometimes I like to think I'll get a second chance if I don't do everything right this time around. I guess we'll never know for sure."

Lana sat quietly, lost in her thoughts.

"Two people tonight made a funny comment to me, about you, Lana. You'll laugh, but . . ."

Marge paused, waiting for Lana's curiosity to take over.

"What's that?" Lana *did* want to know what someone had said about her.

"They said you look just like they picture the princess Urbena looking. So maybe *you* have come back, Princess. Isn't that funny?"

"I — I guess so." Lana would have enjoyed the idea more, earlier in the evening. She wasn't so sure now. She thought about telling Marge what had happened, about the whispering, and someone actually calling her Princess. But she knew Marge would laugh and tease her. Surely the whispers were her imagination.

Arriving at her house kept Lana from saying anything more about the evening. Lana lived close to the museum. Usually she would have walked home, but an early fall snow had left the streets sloppy, and it was unusually cold for October. She jumped out of the car. "Thanks, Marge." She slammed the car door.

Marge waited until Lana reached her front door and had it open. Then she honked and waved. Lana waved back.

"How was the evening, Lana?" her mother called from the living room where she sat watching TV. "There was a mention of the exhibit on the news, and they said they'd have a special segment tomorrow. Did you get your picture taken?"

"No, Mom. Reporters were there, but they only photographed a few of the relics. The party was great." The reception *had* been fun, until the end. Lana would remember the earlier part. She'd forget her flight of fantasy. She was laughing at herself, already.

Trying to laugh. The voice had been so real. She *knew* she had heard something. She wasn't one to invent silly, scary scenes like lights going out and mummies talking to her.

"The teakettle is hot," her mother said. "I made myself a cup of cocoa. Want one?"

"That's exactly what I need." Lana hurried into the tiny kitchen of their cozy house, picked out her favorite mug — the one with funny penguins on it — and stirred up the sweet chocolate. She dug in a plastic bag for two puffy marshmallows, tossed them into the cup, and watched them bob and melt across the top of the hot drink. She'd earned this treat tonight. The party marked the beginning of a great four weeks, even though she was going to have to work really hard to keep up her schoolwork along with guiding people through the museum exhibit after school and on weekends.

Entering her bedroom and snapping on her light, she nearly dropped the small tray with her cocoa and three butter cookies she'd added for further treats.

"Mom," she called. "Who's this?"

Her mother followed her into the room. "I knew you'd be surprised. That's why I didn't tell you."

"But — " Lana stared. A slender black cat stood, stretched, and sat tall like an Egyptian statue on the foot of her bed. He matched the inexpensive cat statue on her bedside table. Two bright yellow eyes stared at Lana, and if cats could smile, this one did, just slightly.

"You wanted a new cat, didn't you?" Mom teased.

"Yes, but I didn't think you'd get me one. I thought we'd go together and pick one out." Lana didn't exactly feel disappointed. Her mother had said when she was ready they'd make a trip to the Good Friends' League. Choose a cat, or let one choose them, to help heal the pain of losing their old cat, Muffy, who had died in August. Muffy had lived to be sixteen, just one year younger than Lana, and Lana still missed her terribly. She and Muffy had grown up together.

"I thought we'd have to go looking for one, too, Lana." Her mother circled Lana's shoulders and hugged her tight. "But sometimes I think cats choose us. I heard this plaintive noise outside the door right after you left tonight. When I opened the door to see what the fuss was, he trotted right in and headed for your room. He's been asleep on your bed ever since."

"How strange." Lana walked slowly toward the cat. She reached out her hand for the cat to sniff.

"Cats are strange. There must have been a sign on our door that said *New Cat Needed Here*. He seemed to know he'd be welcome."

"You think he belongs to someone in the neighborhood and got lost and cold tonight?" Lana didn't want to get attached to the beautiful animal and then find he already had an owner.

"That's possible, but he surely feels at home. Let's deal with that later."

The slim cat stood and rubbed back and forth on Lana's outstretched fingers. Then he stretched, rolled over, and exposed his belly for Lana to rub. The act was one that signaled trust, unusual behavior for a new acquaintance.

Lana sat on the bed and rubbed the soft, silky fur. Soon the cat was on his feet, eager for Lana to love him. She gathered him into her arms and rubbed the top of his head, then his chin. Oh, that felt so good, he said with more purrs, padded his front feet up and down on her knees. What her mother called making biscuits.

Leftover chills from the evening disappeared. "I needed you, Mister," she said to the cat.

Mrs. Richardson smiled at the pair of them. "I never saw a cat take to anyone so fast, Lana. What will you call him?"

Lana pushed aside the idea that this animal might be someone else's pet. "He's obviously an Egyptian cat, worthy of being worshiped. I'm going to call him Seti, after the king who was father to Rameses II."

"Why not Rameses?"

"Ummm, that doesn't seem right for him."

The cat looked at Lana as if thinking about the name — whether he liked Seti. Whether the name was kingly enough.

"Seti, Seti," Lana repeated. "Like it?"

Seti purred and started to curl up in Lana's lap.

"Okay, you do. But let me get in bed before you settle down for another nap, Seti. I'm exhausted."

"There will be huge crowds at the museum tomorrow, Lana. Better go right to sleep." Mrs. Richardson turned to leave the room.

"Don't worry, Mom. There's no way I'm

going to lie awake tonight, even with my being this excited."

Lana pulled on her pajamas and slipped into bed. She drank her cocoa, nibbled her cookies, and looked at Seti, who watched her the whole time. The cat, small for a male, sat tall and regal, looking exactly like one of the ebony statues in the exhibit. Lana reached out for him, but he stepped back, as if to say, don't bother me, I'm busy doing my king-of-the-household look. Just look and worship me.

"You know you're beautiful — handsome — don't you, Seti?"

Seti meowed softly. Yes, of course.

Laughing, Lana smiled and enjoyed looking at her room, which she had decorated in total Egyptian style. Her mother had let her paint a frieze around the ceiling to match those found in tombs and temples. All areas of Egyptian life, as well as Egyptian mythology, were depicted. She had carefully copied the pictures from books she had checked out of the library. On the wall that her bed faced, she had gone all out. A huge scene showed a queen being dressed in all her finery. It had taken her one whole summer to complete it.

Lana's mother was wonderful. She had given Lana an allowance for paint and bought her exotically colored and flowing materials at the department store. Lana covered her bed and windows, then hung the cloth from the ceiling behind the bed to make a false canopy. Josh had laughed when he saw her masterpiece, but she didn't care. She was the one who lived there.

He made up for it the next Christmas by giving her a great book on Egypt. For birthdays and holidays, her mother had given her reproductions of Egyptian artifacts — like the cat statue. Holding it in her hand, Lana looked again at Seti. Twins. She liked the warm, furry version best. She placed her hand on the new cat's side, and he murmured softly.

Her cocoa and cookies finished, she sighed, snapped off her bedside lamp, and snuggled into the covers. She felt the cat get up and turn several times, then settle into the small of her back, a slender, warm heater with a soft motor. He was exactly what she needed to balance out the evening, with its mixed experiences. Excitement at the Egyptian exhibit opening, amusement at Dr. Walters' talk, awe at meeting the archaeologist Blair Vaughn, then the strange, unreal whisperings that were surely in her imagination.

She promised herself that she'd forget the last experience and the scare that she'd had because of it. She drifted off, concentrating on only the good things that had happened. But then the first of the dreams came to her.

I am dressed in a white, pleated gown fashioned of sheer cotton cloth, so soft it might have been woven of cobwebs. Jewels rest at my throat like a collection of dewdrops on the soft bodice. Gold bracelets cuff my wrists as well as my ankles.

On my head rests a heavy wig, woven with ornaments. I long to reach up and pull it off, but instead I hold my head high, with the poise that befits a princess on the day before my wedding.

The litter in which I ride sways from side to side as the slaves beneath me carry it on their shoulders. When I arrive at the palace, one kneels and I step on his back, steadied by my handmaiden, then to the soft carpet that has been rolled out as my walkway to the palace garden.

He meets me in the garden, by a willow tree, not our first meeting, but certainly our most important. For tomorrow the royal wedding will take place. Tomorrow I will become his queen.

At first I lower my eyes and stare at the path under my bare feet, the lovely pink flowers and green hedges of the palace garden. Then, feeling his gaze on me, I dare lift my eyes to his.

In his dark brown eyes I see returned all the

love I have come to feel for him. Ours is a love that will be written in the history books, that poets will exclaim about, that will be sung in melodies all over the kingdom.

His love for me is like nothing I have ever felt before. Passion burns in his eyes with such fervor, I am almost frightened by the intensity. His is a love that will last for today, for tomorrow, and for all of eternity.

Chapter 3

When Lana woke the next morning, she had a vague recollection of her dream. She knew she had been in Egypt, but that didn't surprise her since she had done nothing but read, sleep, eat, and live Egypt for months in preparation for the exhibit. What else would she dream about?

Seti stretched and yawned. "I suppose you slept well, your majesty," Lana said, rubbing his head. He jumped off the bed and looked back as if to say, aren't you coming?

"And now you want breakfast? Do make yourself at home, King Seti." Lana grinned, pulled on her robe, and headed downstairs for the kitchen. Her mother had left her a note on the kitchen table.

Have to work today, even though it's Saturday, alas. Happy opening! I fed Seti some tuna, but will stop on my way home and get proper cat food. Please cut his nails so he doesn't scratch my new furniture. Have fun at the museum and don't get too stressed.

"So you ate? And you were going to con me into feeding you again." Lana filled the teakettle and set it on a burner. "You'll lose your slim figure."

Seti didn't look worried about his figure. He washed his face and then proceeded to groom his entire coat. Lana watched him as she ate an egg and drank her tea. Having a cat in the house again felt right. She had missed Muffy something awful.

Seti led the way up the stairs and back to her room, trotting as if he had an important mission today himself. Before she forgot she grabbed him and held him tightly, neatly clipping off the sharp tip of each claw with her fingernail clippers. He wiggled but put up with it. Then while she dressed carefully in black slacks and a red turtleneck, he sat in the window, looking at the birds in the big cottonwood tree. All the early snow was gone, and the sun was shining brightly.

When she was ready to leave, Lana walked over and looked out the window. Seti reached out his paw and patted the glass.

"I don't know if you can go outside. I'll be gone all day. But then you've been living outside by yourself, if you're truly a stray." Lana didn't want to think about someone coming and claiming Seti. She had gotten attached to the sleek black cat in a very short time.

Her mother hadn't much liked it, but Lana had often let Muffy come and go through her bedroom window. The big cottonwood tree was so tempting for climbing. Lana had often scrambled to the top when she was younger.

Tugging the window up to make an opening, agile-cat size, she unhooked the old screen. There was a tear in it, but she didn't want Seti making it bigger. Quicky, Seti slipped through the open window and out the screen. He stepped onto a huge limb of the ancient tree and hunched down over his feet to watch and wait.

Grabbing a lightweight jacket, Lana set out for the museum. She lived just a few blocks away, easy walking distance. Their neighborhood was made up of old homes, most small but brick, two-story. Just a few blocks over was the posh Park Hill neighborhood, more old homes but estate size. Many of Denver's rich lived there.

Lana felt lucky that she and her mother had a house at all, since her father had died when she was very young. Fortunately, her mother was a great money-manager and had made the best of her father's insurance. She felt bad that her mother had to work today. She had counted on her being in one of the first tours.

Thinking about other things, Lana had walked two blocks when she realized that Seti was following her. "Oh, no, Seti, you can't go with me." She glanced at her watch, scooped up the cat, and ran back. Seti complained about the bouncy ride, but she didn't care. He shouldn't be such an explorer. Thank goodness she hadn't gotten all the way to the museum before she saw him.

While she didn't have to cross Colorado Boulevard, the streets were busy enough. He wouldn't be safe roaming so far from home. Unlocking the front door, she tossed Seti inside, locked up again, and ran. So much for his dignity.

She was hot and sweaty when she reached the museum, just the bad start she needed today. Marge was in the bathroom. She laughed when Lana flew in.

"Don't tell me you overslept. You've been looking forward to today for months."

"No, never mind. It's a long story." Lana dabbed at her face and neck with a wet paper towel. Fortunately her eyebrows and lashes were so dark she didn't have to wear any mascara that would have run. She brushed her shiny hair and let it swing back and forth to fall in place. "No one will look at me anyway."

"Want to bet?" Tugging on her special, ornate vest of red, black, and gold that the volunteers would wear, Marge led the way to the upstairs hall where the Egyptian exhibit had been set up. Lines were already forming, waiting for the doors to open. The guard let Marge and Lana slip into the big front room.

"Lana, hi. I wondered where you were." A tall, dark-haired boy with brown eyes smiled at Lana.

"Rodney, hi. Can you believe that as excited as I am, I was almost late? I have a new cat, and it was his fault."

"Sure, blame it on some innocent animal." Rodney grinned, his picture-perfect teeth white against his tanned face. He and his family had made a return visit to Egypt in late September, so Rod's dark skin was even darker.

For years his parents had worked for the World Health Organization, and Rod had grown up in Cairo. Talk about someone who knew a lot about Egypt's history. Lana had known Rod for a couple of years, but the first time he'd been friendly to her was while they'd been in training for working at the museum. In fact, he'd been so friendly of late that Josh was jealous. Usually she ignored Josh when he had a spell of jealousy. She liked to talk to Rod and, to tell the truth, his attention flattered her. He seemed so sophisticated and worldly. How often could one say, "Well, when I was in Cairo — "

"Have lunch with me at the T-Rex?" Rod invited. "We're on the same schedule."

Lana noticed that he'd taken time to check. That made her feel good, too. "Sure, that would be fun." She smiled at Rod and then took off since she felt her face getting red. How silly. Rod just wanted to be friends, and that was all she wanted. Why was she getting silly about having lunch with him?

Today she was stationed near the case that held the famous necklace. There were other artifacts in the case, but what people wanted to see were the beautiful emeralds that Prince Nefra had given to the princess Urbena for a wedding present. Had she gotten to wear them or had she waited until after the wedding, which never took place?

Lana stared at the necklace while the first tourists were heading her way. She imagined the collar of jewels around her own neck. She could feel the weight, how proud she would have been to wear it.

Her heart went out to Nefra, to Urbena. Their tragedy was one like Romeo and Juliet's.

She hoped, in some other life, they would get back together.

Near the jewelry display case were the mummies. Lana found it interesting to see how people reacted when they saw Nefra. Some stepped back in horror. Some leaned closer with curiosity. She heard bits and pieces of Rod's spiel about preparing a body for burial. He knew all the details. And he hadn't learned it in the last month from reading. Not only had he visited all the pyramids and tombs in Egypt, but he had taken some classes at the museum in Cairo. His research had been firsthand. Once she glanced up to see him staring at her. She waved. He waved back and smiled. His handsome face, his dark eyes on her, sent goose bumps up and down her arms.

"This necklace was Prince Nefra's wedding present for his bride." She started her talk for people standing near the case so she could forget Rod. "Each of the emeralds is perfect. They were probably mined in Zimbabwe or India."

"How much is the necklace worth?" a woman asked.

"Perfect emeralds are as costly as diamonds. I'd have to say it's priceless, since the piece is one of a kind and irreplaceable."

Lana lost herself in telling museum guests about the artifacts. Soon she forgot Rod.

But once, during a slack in the lines of people enjoying the opening day of the exhibit, she noticed that Rod had taken a break. Quickly she slipped over to visit Nefra, who had been tugging at her mind — and her heart — all morning. She wouldn't admit it to anyone else, but she was halfway in love with the image of this young king-to-be.

She was also far enough from her scare last night to look the case over carefully for anything suspicious. Could someone have been playing a trick on her? While someone could have accidentally turned the lights off, thinking everyone had left, the voices she was certain she had heard were not accidental.

There were a myriad of closets and storage bins in the walls around the room. Someone could have hidden and come out into the darkness.

Bending, she checked all around the sides of the coffin. She knelt and looked underneath. If anyone caught her, she'd pretend she'd dropped something. She even ran her hands along the bottom of the coffin, looking for a wire or a microphone. She had no idea why anyone would play such a trick on her, but the more she thought about it, the more she was convinced that the voice calling to her was a childish prank.

She found nothing suspicious. She stood, meaning to take her own break. But before she left the room, she glanced at Nefra once more.

She blinked her eyes. Squinted them together and blinked again. This was impossible. She had memorized this mummy. She was absolutely certain that he lay on his back with one hand over his chest. That was standard mummy posture for a prince.

She stared. Nefra's hand was no longer wrapped and crossed over his chest. Both hands rested alongside his body, one on either side.

Chapter 4

Icy fingers clutched Lana's chest as she stared at Nefra. She struggled to breathe. This couldn't happen. A mummy *moving* wasn't possible. Her mind reeled in a swirl of confusion, then thoughts stalled as if wrapped in cobwebs. One hand was crossed over his chest before, wasn't it? She tried to bring up an image of Nefra when she first saw him. She had looked at him a dozen times. She couldn't remember.

Forcing her eyes from the mummy, she glanced quickly around the museum. Where was Rod? Why was he taking so long with his break? He'd remember. He'd love to tell her she was crazy.

She'd get someone else. Someone very familiar with the relics. It took all her strength to move away from the coffin, as if the air around her had turned to syrup. Placing both hands in front of her, she clawed it away until she escaped. Then she flew to the front door of the exhibit.

"Antef, please, you must come with me." She grabbed the arm of the young man who had traveled from Egypt and across the United States with this collection. He would know.

Antef stared at Lana, a question on his face. "What's wrong, Lana? Your face is as white as my galabiya."

Antef Raam often dressed totally in white. When Lana met him, her first impression was that he was vain and enjoyed getting attention. His face was classic Egyptian. His flawless skin was a smooth medium brown. His eyes dark brown, almost black. He smiled a great deal, but that expression seemed for show, as if he wanted to please everyone, not out of genuine friendliness but for his own gain.

Despite this front he put up, Lana liked the man. She suspected that underneath he was naive and a bit overwhelmed by the United States. He was really very young for the responsiblity he carried. Perhaps he got the job through relatives or knowing someone high up in Egyptian archaeological circles.

He seemed genuinely worried right now. Lana didn't answer him, but took his arm and tugged him back to Nefra's coffin.

"His hands — " She looked at the mummy.

One hand was crossed over his chest, just as she remembered from the first time she'd seen him. A cold breeze swirled around the body as she reached out as if to touch him.

Antef took her arm. "Not a good example for the tourists, Lana. If you want to touch Nefra, it is permitted, but only in private, after museum hours."

Lana didn't want to touch the gauzy linen wrappings. Her hand had moved in disbelief. She backed away, feeling terribly foolish.

"What's wrong, Lana?" Antef repeated. "Why did you come for me? You would like to accompany me to lunch in your strangely named cafe?" He grinned at her and his black eyes teased.

Lana shook her head to clear her thoughts. "I — I — you're going to think me one more crazy American, Antef, but — " Maybe she shouldn't try to explain. She should make up some problem that now seemed solved. But how could her eyes play such tricks on her? "Promise me you won't laugh, Antef, but I'm absolutely sure — well, Nefra's hands and arms were alongside his body a few minutes ago. And I was sure *this* was the way he was when he came in, with one hand crossed over his chest." She pointed to Nefra, looking at the mummy again.

Antef didn't laugh. In fact, he looked a bit frightened. He stared at the mummy, too. "I think you have been in this room too long, Lana. It is time for your coffee break. It will be my honor to treat you. I would like some refreshment, too, even though American coffee is too — too tame for me."

Lana smiled, trying to change her mood. Antef spoke with a slight accent, his English often formal, and occasionally amusing. "I think you mean weak. Tame is for animals. Let's get you an espresso at the T-Rex." She took Antef's arm again and steered him out of the exhibit.

"I am sorry my English is inadequate."

"Antef, your English is wonderful. Do you hear *me* speaking Arabic?" Lana admired anyone who spoke two languages. She had been told that Antef spoke four.

He was small-boned and two inches shorter than she. For a moment she felt she was with a child playing dress-up. Then Antef flashed her a smile that was truly male, truly grown-up, and she felt her face heat up. He was no child.

The smell of Antef's aftershave wafted

around them. As usual, Antef had put on too much. Lana could no longer resist mentioning it.

"What aftershave are you wearing, Antef?" She knew the answer. Josh had tried it once.

"It is the Brut." Antef smiled. "It is much cheaper to get here. You like it?"

Lana decided to be honest. "I'd like a little less, Antef. With scents, less is better. Be subtle, use just a hint of the smell."

"Oh, I am glad to know. I will remember." Again the sexy smile.

Antef probably wasn't trying to take Lana's mind off her foolish fright, but he was doing a good job anyway.

They made their way through the crowded exhibit and out into the third-floor hall of the museum. Now she spotted Rod. She had dropped Antef's arm, but he had taken hers.

"Rod, where've you been? I left a lot of things unguarded."

"I know, Lana, I'm sorry. I was delayed. And I can't have lunch. Another day." Rod offered no excuse for his overly long break or canceling their lunch date, but jogged off to return to the exhibit.

"Your boyfriend?" Antef asked.

"No. My boyfriend doesn't like archaeology. He calls the relics 'old stuff.'" Lana wanted

Antef to know that she did have a special friend.

"In my country we learn better from the time we are very young. We have great respect for the possessions of our ancestors."

"Did you always want to work for the museum?"

"Yes, my father was a guard at the Cairo Museum for all his life. I have this same ambition, since I am not smart enough to be an archaeologist."

"Don't tell yourself that," Lana looked at him to see if he meant what he said. This was the first time she had heard him let down the cool image he had portrayed.

"It is true. I am not good at the schooling. So I work hard to learn about the collection."

"And speak four languages."

Lana didn't know much about Antef's background. Now she realized he was a guard who had a lot of pride. This was why he put up a front. He needed to feel important.

"That was why I came to you, Antef. I knew you were an expert on the relics that came to America."

"I am no help when one's imagination runs away like a speed train." He grinned at Lana and she grinned back. Feeling foolish, but relieved, she continued to laugh and be entertained and to enjoy not only a cup of strong tea but a sticky bun. Antef himself had a sweet tooth and some money to spend, so she let him treat her, and she tried to be good company.

Suddenly she truly wanted to know more about him, to know more about life in modern Egypt. She knew all this history but nothing about what the country was like today. Here was a chance to learn and to help Antef feel good about himself at the same time. Also a chance to take her mind off being so ridiculous this morning.

The rest of the day was busy, crowded with museum viewers wanting the first look at the relics, asking a million questions. She was hoarse by late afternoon. Since she had worked the early shift, she was free at five. Even so, if she hadn't been so exhausted, she wouldn't have wanted to leave. Then, taking off her vest and grabbing her jacket, she remembered she had a date with Josh. How was she going to be scintillating for another four hours?

The sky had clouded over and a cool breeze swept the grounds of the park around the museum. She ran out the back door and cut across the grounds to the back gate. This would save her a couple of blocks of walking. If she hurried home, she might get a half-hour nap that would refresh her.

In the first shadow cast by a huge maple tree, she almost tripped across the black cat. "Seti! What are you doing here?" She bent and scooped the cat into her arms. "Don't tell me you followed me after all and have been waiting all day."

Seti looked at her, and she was sure he smiled. Unlike most cats, who hate to be carried, he curled into her arms and enjoyed the ride home. Lana didn't know what to think. She kept talking to the animal as if he could understand.

"You can't do that, Seti. Cats don't do things like that, follow people and wait for them. Dogs might, but even a dog would probably have gotten bored and gone back home. Did you know how to get home? Maybe that's how you got lost the first time. You followed someone, and they didn't find you again."

Lana stopped abruptly. Seti was purring. "You aren't listening to me." She held the cat up until they were face-to-face. "No, Seti. No. You must not follow me to the museum or anyplace else. A lot of people are superstitious, afraid of black cats. Someone could hurt you, on purpose. Do you understand?"

Seti meowed, actually meowed. But did he meow because that's what cats do? Or because he was saying he'd never, never do this again. Who knows? Lana let out a deep sigh and held the furry body tight again. Did she want another cat? It was so sad to love an animal and then have it die.

Tears ran down her cheeks. Tears for Muffy. Tears for Seti. Tears because she was exhausted. It had been an exciting, upsetting day. Maybe she had already been worn out when she hallucinated that Nefra had moved — had gotten tired of lying in one position for thousands of years, and had shifted into another.

Seti meowed and wiggled to remind Lana that she was holding him too tight. She was comforted by his soft, silky fur against her cheek, his warm, wiry body.

"I love you, Seti, already. Would you please, please be careful? It's too late for me to back out. I'm taking a chance on your being my cat. I'm taking a chance on loving you. Don't let me down."

She ran, tears blurring her path. She needed to hurry home. Needed to feel safe for them both.

Chapter 5

By the time Josh came to pick her up, Lana felt a little better. Her mother had stopped for pizza on her way from work, and Josh arrived early, so it didn't make sense for them to stop for food before the movie.

"I bought Little Caesar's so we could get two," Mrs. Richardson argued. "Save your money, Josh. I'll go watch the news if you two want to be alone."

"Don't be silly, Mom." Lana got out plates and set the table for three. She smiled at Josh. He liked her mother. He'd said so many times.

"Did you see Lana's new cat?" her mother said, sitting down and reaching for the pizza box.

"You get a kitten, Lana?" Josh asked, taking two slices of pepperoni himself.

Lana stared at Josh and wondered what he'd think about Seti coming to them. He wasn't one to believe in anything out of the ordinary. "No, a stray showed up at the door the other night. You know Mom. She took him in. He's upstairs taking a nap. Do you know that he either stayed at the museum all day, Mom, or came over and met me when I got off."

Josh frowned. "And how did he know where you worked?"

Josh Benson was terribly cute when he had that skeptical look on his face, which was often around Lana, since she would be the first to admit that strange things always happened to her. Nothing as strange as what had happened at the museum, she thought, but she wasn't going to tell him, or her mother, about Nefra getting tired of holding his arms in one position.

Josh had white-blond hair, which he wore slightly long and shaggy, the bluest eyes, almost turquoise, and a square, chiseled face that suggested some Viking ancestors. People often commented on the contrast between Lana and Josh when they were together.

Tonight he wore a blue pullover sweater that set off his coloring. If her mother wasn't at the table, Lana would have leaned over and given Josh a kiss. She had missed him, working so many hours to learn the exhibit and as much as possible about Egyptian kings and queens, not to mention gods and goddesses.

Josh never studied a lot, just enough to get by. His passion was golf, and he was on the team at school. He'd probably end up in some public relations work, since he was really good at talking to people and persuading them to do things. Or politics. He was president of the senior class, not to mention several other social organizations.

"Are you staring at me?" Josh asked, grinning at Lana.

"Of course. I like to look at you. Does it bother you?"

Before Josh could answer, Mrs. Richardson took them back to the earlier topic of conversation — Seti. "I'd like to hear the answer to the question about Seti," Mrs. Richardson repeated. "How *did* Seti know to come to the museum?"

"He's a psychic cat," Lana teased, then added, "I'm sure he followed me this morning. I brought him back once, but he must have gotten out and caught up again. I was late so I never noticed the second time." Lana realized her mother was going to ask how Seti got out after Lana brought him home. He'd be grounded for sure.

Seti came into the kitchen then, distracting Mrs. Richardson from asking or thinking about his escape. He meowed by his dish, looking from Lana to her mom. Then he stared at Josh.

"Josh, meet Seti," Lana introduced. "Seti, this is my friend Josh. I hope you'll like him."

"He'd better." Josh pulled a string of cheese from his pizza and held it near the floor. Seti stared at him.

"You know, Lana, this is an unusual cat." Lana's Mom got up and emptied some cat food into a bowl. "He's more — more — well, it seems like a strange word, but sophisticated. Muffy was sweet but really quite a ditz. This cat seems so smart."

"I've heard that a lot of pure black cats are part Siamese." Lana watched Seti eat daintily. "They're smart."

"He knew the house where he'd be treated like royalty." Josh gave up trying to get Seti to be friendly. "He'll probably get more attention than I do."

Josh had complained about Lana's schedule, but she had explained how important the exhibit was to her, so he'd tried to be a good sport.

"Okay, I was going to stay home with Seti, but if you're going to gripe and groan, I guess we'd better go to the movies." Lana collected the plates and put them in the dishwasher.

"I'll cat-sit." Mrs. Richardson laughed.

"Don't worry about us. Right, Seti?"

Seti looked at them, then back at his food. He reached into his dish and lifted out a tiny, crunchy bit with one curled paw. Then he placed it in his mouth.

"Good grief," Josh pushed Lana out the door. "That's picky. I think you have your hands full with that animal."

Lana would have liked to stay home with Seti. She'd never seen a cat do that. Seti definitely wasn't just *any* cat.

The movie was laughing-out-loud funny, and Josh went out of his way to be charming, so Lana let go of everything except being with him. All thoughts of Egypt and mummies, "old stuff," got pushed to the back of her mind.

It all came right back, though, when they stopped for Cokes afterward. They had just gotten seated at TGIF when Rodney Newland came in with a small beautiful girl on his arm.

"Isn't that the guy you've been talking to so much lately?" Josh asked, calling Lana's attention to the couple. He probably wanted Lana to see that Rod had a date with a knockout of a female. "Who is that girl?"

"She's one of the new foreign exchange students," Lana said, staring. "Darrah something — I can't remember her last name. She's from

Cairo, so she probably feels right at home with Rod. He lived there for a long time."

"The student council voted to give the exchange students a party. Maybe I'd better meet her." Josh looked at Lana, probably wanting her to be jealous.

"Good idea." Lana didn't play his game, but did something that was out of character for her. She called across the room. "Rod, Darrah, come and join us."

Rod looked surprised but started toward their table. Darrah's reaction was harder to read, but Lana got the idea she wasn't pleased to share Rod. She didn't smile or act friendly.

Rod introduced her. "Lana, Josh, this is Darrah Bey. She's recently come over from Egypt as an exchange student."

"Welcome to America, to Denver, Darrah. Do you speak English?" Josh asked.

"Of course." Darrah seemed offended. "I've studied English since I was a child."

"Oh, sorry." At least Josh knew how to explain his blunder immediately. "Americans are so language-poor. It's our loss to speak only English."

"Rod lived in Cairo. Do you speak Arabic, Rod?" Lana asked. That was one of the things she'd never gotten around to asking him.

"Badly. I can get along if I have to. In the

school I attended, we spoke English." Rod smiled at Darrah, and Lana found she was a little jealous herself. How strange. She'd been talking to Rod a lot, but she hadn't realized she liked him as more than a friend.

"I'm working in the Egyptian exhibit at the museum," Lana said to Darrah. "Everything about your country fascinates me."

"You're the one Rod has told me so much about," Darrah said, staring at Lana. "The one who looks like an ancient Egyptian."

Lana found she was embarrassed to be the center of attention because of the way she looked. This was certainly not a comfortable foursome. Inviting Rod and Darrah over was probably a mistake. But now that she had, and since they were still standing, Lana said, "Would you like to join us? We're just getting Cokes. We've been to the movie."

"I'd like to hear your impressions of America," Josh added. "Not that Denver represents America very well. I guess I should say your impressions of Denver."

"You would not like what I have to say." Darrah didn't sit down. "I can see that Americans are very spoiled. You all have so much. This is not true in my country."

Even Josh didn't have anything to say to that. Lana knew she and her mother were comfortable, but certainly not rich. She wasn't about to apologize for what they did have because her mother worked very hard.

"Thanks," Rod said, possibly embarrassed by the way Darrah was acting. "But we haven't had dinner. And I have a lot of things to talk to Darrah about. Okay with you, Darrah?"

"Yes, of course." Darrah led the way toward another table.

"Nice girl," Josh said, when they were out of hearing.

"I don't know if exchange students are supposed to be representatives of their country, but if so, she flunks graciousness, doesn't she? It's too bad. She's so attractive."

"She's beautiful. Maybe she's just homesick in a strange place. Maybe she'll get used to us all being rich."

Josh worked at the country club in order to play golf, and he held down a part-time job at Blockbuster Video to buy his clothes and other needs. He was the oldest of five kids, and all those old enough had jobs.

"And spoiled," Lana added. "I've known for a long time that you were spoiled, Josh Benson. She didn't tell me anything new."

"Are you working at the museum tomorrow, Miss Smart Mouth?" Josh took her hand and put his arm around her since he had slid in beside her in the booth. "I could start teaching you to play golf. It's the sport of choice for the rich and famous," Josh joked.

"Sorry, I'm working the afternoon shift. And sometime tomorrow I have a term paper to write. No need to panic, though. It's not due until Tuesday."

Josh laughed. "How could I be crazy about someone who thinks more of dusty old mummies than she does me?"

"I don't know. You're just lucky, I guess."

"I suppose I'd better take you home. Seti is probably waiting up for you."

"He'd better be."

Just for meanness, Lana waved good-bye at Rod and Darrah. Darrah frowned and didn't respond, but Rod waved back.

"Did I ever tell you that the ancient Egyptians worshiped cats?" Lana asked as Josh helped her into his old Mazda.

Josh got in the driver's seat and started the car before he answered. "Do you know the statistics about how much cat food Americans buy a year? I'd say we have a little cat worship going on ourselves. We are a strange bunch. Darrah has that right."

Lana looked, but couldn't see her bedroom window when they pulled in the drive. The idea of Seti waiting up for her had caught her imagination.

When Josh kissed Lana good night, she heard Seti meow immediately. The black cat blended in perfectly with the shadows on the front porch of the Richardson home. Seti perched on a wicker chair cushion and stared at them both. After he had spoken his piece, he jumped down and scratched on the front door, wanting to go inside.

"If I didn't know better, Lana, I'd say he was jealous." Josh pushed Lana toward the door. "You'd better go inside with him before I get scratched."

If Lana didn't know better, she'd think Josh was right. She opened the front door for Seti. He bounced inside, then turned to see if she was following . . . waiting.

Chapter 6

The next day after lunch, Lana made sure Seti was sound asleep on her bed before she left for the museum.

Twice, walking toward the museum, she looked back to be sure he hadn't woken up and followed her. She saw no sneaky black shadow darting from tree to tree, bush to bush. "Silly, silly, silly," she told herself, then turned her mind to today's job.

She would work from two until six, since the museum closed early on Sunday. Maybe, just maybe, she could finish her term paper tonight. Her mother had agreed to her taking on the extra work only if Lana's grades stayed decent. She had never insisted that Lana make straight A's, but Lana knew college was going to depend on scholarships, so no one had to remind her that the top students got the money to go on with their education.

She had to go to college in order to become an archaeologist. There was no question about that. And she *had* to become an archaeologist. She had never wanted to do anything else. She knew jobs were hard to get, that it was a risky career, but she also knew that if you wanted to be happy in life, you had to follow your dreams.

She pushed through the heavy doors at the museum, glancing up at the Tyrannosaurus rex skeleton hanging suspended from the ceiling. There were long lines at the museum box office, and lines in front of the exhibit. A lot of people disagreed with Josh about seeing old stuff. A lot of people would wait an hour or more to see the Egyptian relics.

Rod wasn't working. Neither was Marge. The only person she knew who was there today was Antef. He was talking to a group of people when she slipped into her vest and took her assigned place — the case with the wedding collar. She hoped she could move around, since she took free moments to study the cases herself. She certainly had this one memorized.

The strange, magnetic pull from the mummy was there again. She felt silly — and a little frightened — but Nefra made her feel so special. He made her want to be with him. She stopped at his coffin on her way across the second room. One hand was crossed over his chest. Breathing a sigh of relief, she took time to stare at the mummy for a few minutes and to look at the beautiful face on the coffin lid. She could barely take her eyes off it.

A cloud of warm air surrounded her, bringing a strong feeling of love and well-being. It was the same feeling she'd had after her dream the other night, but this was more overpowering. She walked to the necklace case feeling an intense but painful joy. She finally realized she had a smile on her face when everyone who came along smiled back.

"They should let *you* wear that necklace, young lady," an elderly man suggested. "It would suit you well."

She felt her cheeks heat. "Thank you, sir, but I'm afraid it's much too valuable for that. It is lovely though, isn't it?"

He agreed and stayed for several minutes looking at the jewels. Then he waved with two fingers and moved on.

Late in the afternoon, people came into the show carrying umbrellas, so Lana knew it was raining outside. Inside, the lights had come on early. She was going to get wet going home, since it had never occurred to her that the fall sunshine wasn't going to last.

Despite a snack on her break, Lana was hungry. Without looking at her watch she knew that it was almost six o'clock. She did check. A quarter to. There were only a young couple and two elderly men still in her room. The other volunteer had left, but Lana felt that she should wait until all the people were gone.

She turned to check the area behind her when the lights went out. Remembering what had happened the last time, she froze. Her knees started to tremble, her heart beat faster, and her pulse throbbed. She waited for the whispering to begin. She wished she had something to hold onto.

Suddenly someone bumped into her. "Hey — " she called out. Then a hand shoved her and she stumbled, falling onto the floor before she could catch herself.

Immediately she was on her feet and shoving back. She moved with good instinct and took hold of whoever this was. He or she pushed Lana again but Lana was ready this time. She struggled to grasp something on the person, hold on until she could catch her breath and yell for help.

"Help — he — " Someone's hand closed over her mouth before she could call loudly. "Let me go," she muttered into the sweaty palm, but it came out like a muffled stutter.

Her arms flapped and slapped but she couldn't get a grip on the person or his clothing. She grabbed again before he hit her shoulder and shoved her harder. This time she skidded to the floor, dazed.

A crash exploded the case near her, sending splinters of glass in all directions. Instinctively, she spun around, her back to the noise, but one sliver shot into her arm with a piercing pain. She heard footsteps crunching on the glass, then running away.

As she sat up, the lights flickered and came back on. She blinked to focus and glanced all around her. No one. She was alone in the room.

Her arm was bleeding slightly, but when she pulled out the sliver of glass, a stream of blood flowed and dripped onto the floor. She slipped the object in her hand into the pocket of her vest. Then quickly she reached into the waistband of her slacks and pulled out a tissue she had tucked there. She pressed it over the wound with the thumb and finger of her left hand and held it tightly.

A regular museum guard, a man assigned to the exhibit, and Antef reached her at the same time.

"Lana, what happened? You are hurt. Let me see." Antef knelt beside her.

"I'm fine, Antef. A small puncture is all. See what — "

Antef helped her to her feet. She could see for herself what had broken. The case with the wedding collar. The necklace with the beautiful, large emerald that symbolized the eye of Osiris, god of the underworld.

"The necklace, Antef," she whispered, moving closer, kicking aside the broken glass. *"The wedding necklace is gone!"*

Chapter 7

Biting her lip and holding back the tears, Lana stared at the shattered case. Whoever had hit the glass had done so carefully. Only the side where the necklace rested was broken. She took a quick inventory of the rest of the contents.

"Nothing else is missing. There's the carnelian cat statue, the bowl of hammered copper, and the faience glass-paste beads." She moved around a little, glass crunching under her shoes. "The fish amulets are there, the gold earrings." She pointed as she itemized the collection she had been in charge of, the one she had memorized by standing there for two work sessions.

"I would have to say that the thief was certainly bold, breaking into the case while people were here, thinking he could escape with the necklace," commented the one remaining man who was looking at the exhibit.

"He must still be in the museum," Lana said, realizing that they should close all the exits. "Has anyone called the police?"

"Of course." Antef looked at Lana's arm. "You need a doctor."

"No, I don't. Look, my arm has already stopped bleeding." Lana pulled away the tissue. There was only the small red spot where the glass had pierced her skin in a shallow wound. "There are first-aid supplies in the office. I'll get some antiseptic and a Band-Aid in a minute."

Antef hurried away to get those things for her. The museum security guard came back, followed by Dr. Walters.

"Lana, fortunately I was still here. What happened?"

"It was all so fast," Lana explained. "The lights went out and I struggled with someone."

"Do you know who it was?" Dr. Walters frowned.

"No, it was dark. I couldn't even tell if it was a man or a woman, but the person was strong. He, or she, shoved me down and then broke the case. It took only seconds to grab the necklace and run."

"Was it insured?" The stranger watched beside them, not exactly acting like an innocent bystander.

"Yes, of course, but that doesn't matter. The piece is not replaceable. We can't even really put a value on it."

All of a sudden Lana found herself surrounded by people. Blair Vaughn was the first to speak. "You let someone steal the wedding necklace, Lana?"

"Well, I — "

"Lana didn't *let* someone steal the necklace, Blair." Dr. Walters spoke in a stern tone of voice. "This is not her fault."

If anyone wanted to make Lana feel guilty, it wouldn't be hard. She kept thinking she should have been able to stop the theft. She *had* had hold of the thief.

"Did you call for security immediately?" Blair asked, continuing to question Lana in an accusing voice.

"I don't know. It all happened so fast. I tried to yell. I tried to stop him, but I couldn't. And the lights were off. I didn't know what was happening. That he planned to steal something."

"Why else would he turn off the lights and push you aside?" Blair stared at Lana, unwilling to let her have any excuses, eager to blame Lana for this terrible loss.

Lana's head throbbed, and she ached all over. But there wasn't time to think that maybe something was hurt more than her pride. She was probably bruised, but her heart ached at the idea of this happening when she was on duty, supposed to be protecting things.

A policeman made her tell her story again. She closed her eyes and related it, trying to live every moment over. Officer Callahan asked things she couldn't remember, though, and soon she felt really confused.

"What kind of clothing was he wearing? How tall was he? Was he fat or thin? Did he have any odor about him?"

Lana kept shaking her head. How was she supposed to take in all that information in a matter of seconds? There was something. She did know *something* else, but it wouldn't come to her.

Finally Officer Callahan said the worst thing of all. "How do we know this happened, Miss Richardson? Maybe you're making all this up."

"You think *I* took the necklace?" Lana stared at him, some of her exhaustion falling away, being replaced by anger. "You think I broke the case and took the collar? What would I do with it? Where is it now?"

"You could have hidden it. Look at all these cupboards. You could plan to take it out of the museum later." Callahan seemed convinced he'd found the answer.

"Wait a minute, officer." Dr. Walters proceeded to set Callahan straight. "Miss Richardson is one of our best volunteers. She's a member of the Egyptian Study Society, a student of Egyptology. You are certainly wrong about thinking she took the necklace."

"She'd know it was the most valuable piece here." Callahan wasn't convinced.

"She's a high school senior, Officer Callahan. Not a thief." Even Blair Vaughn softened toward Lana with Callahan attacking. She had been upset when she first came in and had pointed her finger at the first person she saw. Common sense would have told her later that it wasn't Lana's fault that this had happened. "Come on, Lana, I'll take you home."

"No, I'm fine, Blair. Thanks. You can be helpful to Dr. Walters and the police. They'll want to be sure the necklace is the only thing missing. And you can help them decide how the thief could dispose of the piece. He can't just go out and sell it."

"Are you sure you don't want some company?" Blair took hold of Lana's arm and walked partway to the room for employees and volunteers. "It would help you to talk this out some more. We might think of something you forgot to tell the police."

The museum had been sealed. A few tourists were trapped inside. They were being questioned by the police before they could go home.

"I'm sure. I live very close. I don't want to talk any more. And I'm not hurt. I was fortunate."

"Yes, you were. You could have been badly cut by the glass or knocked out by the thief. He took a big chance to pull this off during hours the museum is open."

Lana watched Blair turn and walk down a back hall toward the museum offices. She mumbled to herself and seemed to be thinking about how this could have happened.

Grabbing her jacket, Lana pulled it on over her vest. She felt cold, so terribly cold. Antef met her as she reached the front door.

"I have not given you this bandage, Lana. Someone stopped me to ask what happened." He held out a paper-wrapped strip.

"Oh, I'd forgotten about it." Lana pulled up the sleeve of her jacket. The small cut had started to bleed again. Antef pulled apart the paper and placed the adhesive strip over the wound. He held this thumb tight on it for a minute.

"Antef, I'm so sorry, so sorry." The idea that she could have prevented tonight's loss flooded over Lana again.

Antef held on to her arm for a few minutes. His hands were so warm, his eyes so intense. "You cannot worry, Lana. This is not your fault. It is a great loss, but surely we will find the piece. Your police here are very efficient, I think."

"No pawnshop would take the necklace, Antef. The thief could never hope to sell it. If he took it for the money, he may be disappointed."

"This is true. We have photos. The newspapers can publish the photos."

"I have heard that private collectors sometimes buy stolen art pieces only for themselves. But surely — that's so selfish."

"Please, I will worry for you." Antef smiled. "You must not feel bad."

"I do. I can't help it. Your government trusted us to have this show here. This makes our museum look bad." Lana couldn't stop talking.

"I can take you home?" Antef asked. "It is late, and the rain, I think the rain comes."

"No, thank you, Antef, no. I live close." Lana certainly didn't need anyone worrying about her. "You stay here and worry for me." She tried to smile.

At the door, a policeman had to go and get permission from Callahan for Lana to leave. While she waited she hugged herself, feeling colder and colder. She paced back and forth near the gift shop, staying away from the front door opening and closing, as visitors were questioned and allowed to leave.

Finally the young policeman returned and nodded at her. "You may leave, Miss Richardson. Are you all right?"

"Yes, just cold. Thank you." Lana slipped out the front entrance of the museum and hurried away. She debated for seconds whether or not to cut across the park. It was so much closer.

A foggy mist rolled along the lawns and swirled in and out of the trees. The dampness brought with it a silence that spread around her, making her feel isolated, alone in time, caught in some kind of unreal landscape, not of this earth.

In no time she was wet and shivering harder. She had lost her perception of how far she had walked, how much farther it was to the street.

From behind a tree slid a fuzzy vaporous light suspended like a small moon to guide her. That must be the corner of Downing and Seventeenth.

No traffic passed, no sounds reached her at all, making the silence even more frightening. Then the whispering started.

Calling her name. "Lana, Lana. Give it back, Lana."

She whirled around, trying to decide from which direction the voice came.

"What? Give what back?" She knew what.

"Give back my necklace. It is mine."

Lana stopped and stared into the fog, swung around and looked behind her, beside her. Into the huddle of dark trees to her right.

Wisps of fog drifted, formed gray fingers that pulled back curtains of mist to reveal a dark shape. The shadowy figure walked slowly toward her, making a squishy sound in the wet grass. Lana's feet became heavy, as if coated with blobs of mud. Her shoes pulled her legs down, rooted them in place.

She blinked and her eyes focused more and more until she could make out what the figure was.

Before her, not six feet away, stood Nefra. Not the beautiful boy on the lid of the coffin. But the musty-smelling, bandaged, mummified body.

Chapter 8

Her legs drained, going soft and weak. Time became silent seconds. She held her breath until her chest ached.

"Give it back," the mummy whispered again. The voice was the same hoarse whisper of the museum darkness. "Give back the necklace. You are already *cursed*."

Slowly, as if thousands of years had stiffened the arm, one hand rose. One blackened finger pointed.

Lana stepped back.

And back.

And back.

She could not scream, nor speak, nor could she take her eyes from this apparition.

Once more she stepped back. She stumbled and fell backward over something behind her.

Seti!

The cat arched his spine. Fur spiked and

swelled, doubling the cat's small size. A terrible hiss rent the silent curtain of mist that hung over them.

Now the mummy stepped back.

And back.

And back.

On stiffened legs, Seti bounced forward, ready to attack. A yowl started in the back of his throat and swelled to a shriek. Launching himself on catapult back legs, he leaped and tore at the gauzy covering of Nefra's shroud.

No longer stiff, the mummy flung off the cat and fled. Seti didn't chase him, just arched and danced forward a few more feet.

Lana found her voice. "Seti, oh, Seti. Come here, please come to me."

Seti lowered his spiked fur, gave it two swift licks, and walked softly to where Lana sat on the wet grass. He rubbed against her legs, butting his head on her knee, purring as if nothing out of the ordinary had happened. As if tonight was only another stroll in the park to meet Lana and walk her home.

She gathered the warm body to her chest, tucked him under her chin, and took comfort from his familiar company.

"Oh, Seti." She breathed out the words over and over. That was all she could say. Thank you for saving me from the mummy, was much too ridiculous a statement.

Had she imagined the monstrous sight? Was this some bad dream from which she would awake, safe in her bed, Seti curled close to chase away the nightmare?

No. She was still in the park behind the museum. She was sitting on the wet ground. Her pants were fast becoming soaked. Rain fell from the sky now, the mist turning to a steady pour. Uncontrollable shivers told her she must get up and hurry home. She needed a hot shower and — and what? A safe harbor to begin with. Then she'd think about what had just happened. She struggled to her feet and ran.

"Lana, is that you?" her mother called as she stepped inside the front door. "Why are you so late? I was getting terribly worried."

"Oh, Mom, we had an awful night." Lana unloaded part of her story. "Just before closing someone smashed the case where the wedding necklace was on display and took it. Security locked all the doors and the police came and we had to answer all these questions — no one had an answer — but they let people go one by one, hoping to find the thief."

Lana didn't tell her mother that at first they suspected her. Well, maybe they never really thought she took the necklace, but it seemed that way at the time. She was the one closest to it. She could have faked the whole event if she were stupid enough to think she could get away with it.

"You're soaked. Go take a hot shower and get your robe on. I'll heat you some potato soup — I made a pot for supper — and you can talk while you eat." Her mother's face registered surprise at last. "Did — where did you find Seti? I called and called him when it started to drizzle. He didn't — "

"He came to meet me. I don't know how he found his way, but — but — " What she wanted to say was, thank God he did, but then her mother would want to know why she was so relieved to be met by a cat instead of worried about his finding his way to the museum. "But he did. You're right, I have to shower." She fled to her room.

She let the hot water pound on her body until some of the stiffness and cold retreated. Until some of her leftover fear dissolved and floated down the shower drain.

By the time she slipped into her pajamas, bathrobe, and fuzzy slippers, anger had taken the place of fear.

That was *not* the mummy of Nefra who had approached her in the park. Thousand-year-old bodies don't get out of coffins and go walking in the rain.

Someone was trying to frighten her. Someone *had* frightened her. Why? Why would anyone want to do that? The whispers in the dark museum, now this intricate dressing up in order to appear in the mist.

Effective — yes. At the time. In the real world of her home, her exotic, Egyptian-decorated bedroom, not believable. She wasn't some silly schoolgirl who'd be intimidated by theater tricks.

"I can think that now, can't I, Seti?" Lana walked over and picked up the cat, who had taken the opportunity to wash his own wet skin and fur and slick it back into perfect order. He was putting on the last licks when Lana lifted him and hugged him close. "Thank you, thank you again, Seti. I don't know how you knew to come, but I'm glad you did."

Seti got a bowl of warm milk. Lana, a bowl of her mother's delicious and comforting potato, onion, and celery soup. Rich, melted butter floated in golden patterns across the thick, creamy mixture. Bay leaf spiced the soup perfectly. Lana ate the entire bowl and licked her spoon before she spoke.

"Thanks, Mom. That saved my sanity." She

reached for a slice of homemade garlic bread and chewed off a mouthful as her mother refilled the bowl.

"Do they have any idea who might have taken the necklace?" Mrs. Richardson finally asked. Lana knew she had been holding back a million questions.

"No. All they could do was take everyone's name who remained in the museum. The thief could have escaped before they locked the doors. Or he may have hidden it and will go back later when things calm down. They'll keep looking, of course."

Lana told her mother the whole story again from start to finish — well, almost to the end. She didn't add the final drama in the park. She didn't want her mother worried about letting her walk to the museum alone, or come home at night alone. Lana would worry about that enough for both of them.

But if that — that thing tried to frighten her again, she was going to go after it herself, catch whoever thought this was a joke or even felt he was frightening her.

Sure you will. No problem. You are one brave lady, Lana.

Okay, she liked thinking she would. She didn't like someone thinking they could scare her so easily. She wasn't some wimpy little creature who was afraid of every shadow.

"Lana, is anything else wrong?" Her mother was too intuitive. Lana had gotten quiet for too long.

"I'm exhausted, Mom. This has been one long weekend. I'm not going to finish any term paper tonight, either."

"I will refrain from saying anything about leaving it until the last minute." Her mother smiled.

"Thanks, Mom. You're all heart." Lana licked her spoon a second time, and felt comfortably stuffed and warm at last. She sipped the hot tea her mother had poured for her and looked at Seti.

The cat washed his face, licking a paw, swiping it over his cheek and chin, licked again, swiped. He looked like any perfectly ordinary alley cat, but he acted like a person. A very smart and intuitive person. One who was connected —

Seti gave her that look that seemed like a smile again. He knew she was looking at him, thinking about him. He was connected to her mind.

This was a psychic cat. She and Seti had a psychic connection. She picked him up and headed upstairs to read in bed. She didn't know if Seti made her feel safe or uneasy.

The next morning she dressed for school — surely she didn't have to go to school. That was too normal. What she wanted to do was be at the museum when it opened and look everywhere for the wedding necklace. The more she thought about it, the more she was convinced the thief didn't try to take the jewelry out of the museum last night. He'd hid the collar, planning to get it later.

Seti watched her put on jeans and her red sweater over a navy turtleneck. The morning was damp and cold. She had closed her window last night, but her room was icy.

She picked up the still damp, crumpled slacks and blouse from the floor in front of her closet. Her museum vest looked awful. She'd have to hurry home from school and press it before she went to work. Monday. Was she scheduled for Monday? She'd go anyway.

Placing the vest on a hanger, she noticed a lump in the pocket. She put one finger into the shallow opening and came up with a button. She stared at it.

The button matched the buttons on her own vest, but she wasn't missing one. A tiny memory surfaced. She had grabbed at the thief's clothing, trying to hold on to him. She must have torn this button from his vest and then put it in her pocket without thinking when she was trying to stop her arm from bleeding.

So the thief was a volunteer for the Egyptian exhibit. That narrowed the search considerably. He wasn't some person who'd come in as if looking at the relics and then waited for a chance to take the priceless jewelry.

Should she call the police right now and give it to them as evidence? Probably. But she didn't. She wasn't sure why. Instead, she placed it in the small pocket at the waist of her jeans.

The school day seemed endless. At noon, Rod grabbed her and made her tell everything that had happened last night — twice. Darrah approached her in chemistry class and questioned her. She was almost friendly, but then she wanted information. Josh worried about her getting hurt. The incident was over, but she had to talk fast to make him feel better.

Begging Josh to take her home before he went to work, she dashed into the house to press her vest. She had called the museum at noon to ask if she could work extra time, since her schedule revealed she wasn't on today. Mrs. Cocharan said fine, that Dr. Walters wanted to talk to her again anyway.

Making sure her bedroom window was locked tight, and that Seti was asleep on her bed, she slipped out the front door and locked it behind her.

She didn't head straight for Dr. Walters' office, however. She had to look at the smashed display case first. The glass was cleaned up and the case gone, of course. In its place was a smaller case with the treasures the thief had left behind. She stared for a moment at the carnelian cat who sat tall and straight, imitating Seti.

She moved to study a mummified cat, embalmed and wrapped exactly like the human bodies. She knew why these people had worshipped cats. Not just because they saved their crops from rats and mice, but for their mystery. She was fast thinking of Seti as a mysterious animal for whom she had all the respect in the world, more than she did for some humans.

Then she moved to the mummy of Nefra, staring at it for a few moments. She stared at the dark eyes and perfect face on the lid of the coffin. Stared at the empty coffin belonging to Urbena. Somehow she needed to take all this in again even though every piece in the exhibit was etched into her mind and memory.

She took a deep breath, patted the button still in her pocket as she had done every hour all day long. She had better report to Dr. Walters, show it to him, give it to him. He'd know what to do next, to tell the police, talk to each volunteer, or keep the information to himself. She'd rely on him to do what was right and best.

She was having a hard time leaving Nefra's coffin. She felt the strange magnetic pull, the same warmth she often did while standing beside Nefra. The same tug, the pull to meet his mind, even though it had been stilled so many years in the past. Somehow she felt a connection that was as real as today, as real as if the boy-king were standing beside her, about to take her in his arms. She had never before felt this depth of emotion. Her intense feelings moved her to tears.

Admit it, Lana, you are in love with Nefra, a tiny voice inside her said.

She was. She had to admit it. She was in love with the idea of this man, the image — the spirit — of him that seemed so present when she stood beside him. And, romantic that she was, she was in love with the Romeo and Juliet story of Nefra's and Urbena's love and tragic ending.

She knew this young man.

She stood staring at the mummy for the longest time.

"Daydreaming again, Lana?" A voice pulled her back to the present. The strong smell of his aftershave told her who it was. "Perhaps you have a fantasy about the young and handsome king?"

Antef's eyes teased her. She felt a blush heating up her cheeks, since his perception of what she was doing was so much on target. She laughed to cover her embarrassment.

"Antef — " She meant to ask him if anything else had been discovered today. If any more information had been released about the necklace or the thief.

Before she could speak, she noticed that Antef wore the volunteer vest today. She knew he had one but he didn't always wear it, favoring the flowing white robes. But today he was dressed more American style. Jeans, red turtleneck that complimented his dark complexion, and the vest over the shirt. The vest was a bit rumpled as hers had been before she ironed it.

But the detail that had made her blood run cold was that the middle button from the vest was missing.

Chapter 9

"Antef." She took a deep breath. "Antef, you've lost a button off your vest. Did you know that?"

"Oh, so I have." Antef fingered the spot where the button should have been. "I never should have left my vest in the employees' room. It disappeared, and now look at it. Wrinkled and missing a button. Perhaps I can press it, and they will have extra buttons in the office?"

"Perhaps." Lana didn't know whether to believe Antef or not. Her intuition said not, but her common sense said, why would Antef want to steal from the exhibit when he seemed so sincere about people enjoying it, about being a part of it himself? And what could he do with the necklace? He'd have to sell or pawn it in Denver, since he'd never get it back into Egypt in his luggage or on his person.

Memories work in strange ways. As soon as Lana connected the button to Antef's vest, she remembered the other detail of the theft she had been trying to dredge up last night for the police. A smell. When she was struggling with the thief, she'd smelled Antef's aftershave. Surely that smell and the button screamed out that he was the thief. But was it enough to accuse him and make it stick? He's already said his vest was stolen. A lot of people probably wear Brut aftershave. Josh's brother for one. A lot of museum volunteers? The obvious evidence certainly pointed to Antef.

"I — I'm not working today. Dr. Walters wanted to talk to me. I guess I'd better go see what he has to say. Who do you think took the necklace, Antef?" She asked outright, just to see what Antef would say.

"The theft is a puzzle." Antef looked away from Lana. "I do not know what to think."

"That collar is worth a lot more than money. It's one of your national treasures. Irreplaceable. I hope we can find it for you."

Lana left Antef staring at the space on his vest where the button should be. She found it hard to tell what he was feeling or if he realized she thought he had stolen the necklace.

Dr. Walters was on the phone when Lana

got to his office. He waved her to a chair. "Yes, yes, please do. We'll help all we can. We must retrieve this piece. You understand that, don't you?" Walters listened, then said yes again and hung up.

His long, thin face was even longer. Dark circles under his eyes suggested that he hadn't slept much, if at all, since last night's theft.

"I'm so sorry, Dr. Walters. I feel awful to have had this happen while I was working."

"No one ever suspected you, Lana. I hope you know that." He made a pyramid with the fingers from both hands and stared at it as if there were secrets in the formation.

"Dr. Walters, why do you think Blair accused me so quickly?" Lana was really asking to know more about Blair Vaughn. This was a good place to start.

Dr. Walters ran his hand through his hair, as if to give him time to think about what to say. "Miss Vaughn is rather excitable, Lana. Sometimes I believe she thinks all the artifacts in Egypt are her personal responsibility. She's very dedicated to her work."

"But intense." Lana smiled.

"Yes, you could say that." Dr. Walters smiled back. "Although her grandfather had worked in Egypt, her father practically forbade her to go into archaeology. But if you know

Blair, you know telling her *not* to do something makes her want to do it even more. And she's quite a feminist. I have nothing against women in any workplace, but Blair quite often uses being female to take umbrage."

"She did tell me I'd have to work twice as hard as a man to get a good job."

Walters nodded. "I'd say twice as hard as other archaeology students. There are more people, male and female, wanting jobs than there is work. Interesting work."

They sat quietly for a few moments. Lana reached in her pocket. "Dr. Walters, I didn't realize it last night, but I pulled a button off the thief's jacket — vest. I think I put it in my pocket when I was trying to stop my arm from bleeding."

"Is your arm okay?" His attention was on Lana again. He reached out and took the button, stared at it.

"Oh, yes, it was only a small wound from a glass shard. That button is from one of the volunteers' vests. See, it matches mine." She showed him her vest in case he'd forgotten the design.

"One of our own," Dr. Walters said softly. His face got longer and sadder. "I trusted all our volunteers."

"The thief may not be a volunteer, though.

I — don't know what to think of this, but Antef is missing a button from his vest. I saw him just now and asked him about it. He said his vest disappeared yesterday. He'd left it in the employees' room."

Dr. Walters turned the button over and over and over in his fingers. "Don't tell anyone about this, Lana, until I ask some questions myself. Sometimes the police are so heavy-handed. Antef is a guest in our country, and this could be a delicate situation."

Lana wondered whether or not to share the aftershave clue, and all the other things that had happened to her, with Dr. Walters, since he seemed to be taking it on himself to investigate. Would he say she couldn't keep working? She couldn't bear that. She'd wait.

"Well, this is my day off and I have homework. I'd better get home." She stood, and when Walters didn't say anything, she turned and left him with his thoughts and the problem.

Slowly she walked home, covering the same ground as last night, but the rain had wiped out any footprints that she or someone else might have made on the path.

At home, she wasn't able to give full attention to her paper, but she did finish writing it. Maybe it would be all right. Seti watched her work for a short time, then he curled up and went back to sleep. Seeing him so comfortable made her even more exhausted. She suspected that the stress of the night before was catching up with her.

By ten o'clock she was in bed. She fell asleep immediately and in a short time she was dreaming.

Inside the pyramid is dark and cool. A musty smell surrounds me. Not only is the air stale, but there is so little. I have to suck in long deep breaths to keep from feeling dizzy and disoriented.

Carefully I descend the long stairway, bending farther and farther over as the passageway narrows down. I wad my long skirt into one hand to keep from tripping over it. The other hand, pressed against the rough, cold wall to help me balance, carries a small candle. My sandals slap each step as I walk slower and slower. Coming out into a small room, I stare ahead. The candle flame is not much help. My eyes adjust to the dim interior. Deep inside the structure, I reach for the huge double doors, tugging them open. There, in another small room, rests the sarcophagus of Nefra.

I stare at the tomb, overcome by a deep sadness. An ache fills my heart. I kneel and lean my head on the coffin. No tears come. There are none left.

A small shuffling sound comes from behind me. I sit up straight and turn to see what the noise is. Rough hands grab me. A sack is thrown over my head. I struggle until I pass out.

When I come to, I am lying in a cold, dark space. Reaching out, I touch a rough wooden ceiling just inches above my face and my body. I push my hands to both sides. Again there is almost no space. I try to sit up. There is no room.

I am closed in — into a small, contained space. A — coffin. I am inside a wooden box. Then I hear the clods of dirt hit the lid. Pebbles bounce and rattle down the sides.

Someone is filling the space above me. I am buried, buried alive! Almost immediately the air grows stale and close. I choke, try to call out, to scream.

Darkness presses upon me. What little air is left becomes heavy and presses down upon my chest. Down and down and down until I can no longer inhale, exhale. Down and down and down, suffocating darkness. . . . Heavy. . . . Heavy. . . . Darkness.

* * *

Lana clawed her way back to consciousness, to now, to her room, her bed. Seti had curled on her chest, almost under her chin. He was heavy, so heavy. She pushed him aside, sat halfway up, and took long, deep breaths of the sweet, life-giving air around her.

A dream. Only a dream. She shook her head to clear the cobwebs, to come back to this time.

Someone — someone had buried her alive. She shuddered at the idea, the experience her dream had provided, the terror of being confined underground, in that small space, and knowing, knowing she was going to die there.

Who was the girl in the dream? No one had called her name, but if she was mourning over the boy-king Nefra . . .

Did the princess Urbena really commit suicide? Or was she murdered? Buried alive? She died there, and her body wasn't even properly prepared? Perhaps the reason Urbena's mummy hadn't been found was that there was no mummy. Her body had disintegrated and turned to dust.

Lana's imagination took over from where her dream had left off. There was no way to *know* any of what she was thinking. No answers now for the questions.

She snapped on the lamp beside her bed.

Seti closed his eyes, then opened them to tiny slits, watching her.

"Don't sleep on me like that, Seti," she scolded. "You probably helped cause my dream. I couldn't breathe because of you."

He stared at her through golden eyes, his black pupils narrow because of the sudden light.

She reached over and snapped off the light, curled up on her side, and tried to go back to sleep. It took a long time, even with the warmth and comfort of Seti in a soft comma, curled against her stomach.

Unlike some dreams that are gone by morning, some that you want to remember and can't, Lana's dream, the experience, the emotion, stayed with her all day. She wondered what it meant — if anything. Maybe it was just a strange scenario her imagination had conjured up to devil her while she slept.

At lunch, standing at the edge of the cafeteria, tray in hand, she spotted Darrah sitting alone at a nearby table. Darrah might not welcome her company, but Lana would try.

"Hello, Darrah, mind if I sit here?" Lana sat before Darrah could answer. Darrah only nodded and stared at her. Then she went back to eating the spaghetti before her, trying to keep it on her fork and get it to her mouth.

"Some of your food is strange." Darrah almost smiled and Lana felt better. She was glad she'd taken the chance to sit with the girl. "But I like your pizza."

"Are you feeling more at home? I know everything must have seemed strange at first."

Lana studied the Egyptian girl. She had a dark, exotic beauty that was accented by the deep reds and blues she seemed to prefer. Her hair was jet-black, short and curly, almost frizzy. She loved jewelry, obviously, since one ear was pierced three times, the other twice. Long, dangling silver earrings mixed with small beads of jasper and carnelian, hung from the main pierced place. Tiny silver rings circled the other holes. Around her neck Darrah wore beads of carnelian mixed with beads of silver, surely expensive, as well as a small rectangle with her name on it.

Lana reached out and took the necklace in her hand. "This is your name in hieroglyphics? I understand it's lucky to wear your name."

"Yes." Darrah drew back slightly. Lana had intruded too far into her personal space. Lana dropped the charm but didn't apologize.

She pulled out a charm from a chain around her own neck. "I wear an ankh, the key of life.

My boyfriend bought it for me last Christmas."

Darrah played with her lunch again without talking. All of the fingers on her right hand held a ring, three fingers of her left. Lana knew that in India the women wore much jewelry. They wore their wealth instead of using a savings account. She wondered if that same idea prevailed in modern Egypt. It wasn't something she could ask comfortably. There was something else she wanted Darrah's opinion on, though.

"Darrah, I've been having strange dreams. Tell me what you think of them. I'm always in ancient Egypt. I seem to be a princess or a queen by the way I'm dressed. Such strong feelings come with the dreams as if I'm really there instead of dreaming. Last night I woke up frightened because someone was trying to kill me." Now Lana played with her own food.

"There is much mystery in our land," Darrah said. "Much magic. Black magic. Sometimes it is dangerous to delve too deep into those mysteries. This dream may be a message for you."

"What message?"

"One that says you are interfering in something you do not understand. That you should step away from it. There is also much power in our mythology. But misused power is dangerous."

Lana looked straight into Darrah's eyes. "Are you telling me to mind my own business?"

"You have this saying." Darrah smiled, but it wasn't a friendly smile. "If the shoe fits, wear it." She got up and left the cafeteria quickly.

Lana stared at the retreating girl. She felt confused by Darrah's attitude, and her warning, if that was what it was. Her talk of Lana misusing some mysterious power certainly made no sense. Lana felt powerless in what was happening to her. She had no control over her dreams. Her strong feelings for Nefra could probably be explained by an overactive imagination. And her thinking he had moved that one time — well, that was certainly a flight of fantasy. Tired and excited, she had gotten carried away and her eyes had tricked her.

As for someone speaking to her in the dark museum, and then the mummy approaching her in the park, that *had* to be a trick. A prank to frighten her. She didn't know why. It had worked at the time, however, but now, sitting in the high school cafeteria, she could hardly believe that either had happened.

No mystery. No power. Just confusion.

Lana had been so excited about the museum exhibit, the most important event in her whole life. But now that some of the newness had worn off, what was she left with? A very strange and helpless feeling of pieces of her life being totally out of control.

Chapter 10

For a week nothing out of the ordinary happened. Lana daydreamed through five periods at school. She had arranged to get out early every day she worked. She hurried to the museum and watched what seemed like thousands of people stroll through the exhibit — busloads of schoolchildren, vans of senior citizens, young mothers pushing strollers. She talked to them all, answered their questions when she could.

She kept an eye on Antef, who seemed no different, except that he stopped flirting with her. Blair Vaughn came in on that Thursday and stopped to talk to Lana at a slow time.

"You get a coffee break soon?" Blair asked. "I'll treat at the T-Rex."

Since it was quiet, Lana waved to Marge that she was leaving. Marge gave her a thumbs-up okay signal.

Blair was quiet walking downstairs. Selecting an espresso plus a huge piece of carrot cake, she paid for her food and Lana's Coke, then led them to the farthest table in the back hall.

"I apologize for jumping on you the other night, Lana," Blair said, eating the cake out from under the cream cheese frosting. Lana wondered if she was saving it till last or dieting. "I was just so upset that anyone would think of stealing that necklace."

"That's all right, Blair. I was upset, too. At the time everyone was upset, but also everyone was suspect. I didn't take it personally." Lana had taken it a bit personally at first, but once she calmed down she understood.

"I guess I take everything personally." Blair laughed.

Lana felt she had the opening for a more personal statement and maybe a chance to find out more about Blair. "Dr. Walters told me your father didn't want you to be an archaeologist, but that your grandfather worked in Egypt at one time. Tell me about him."

"There's nothing to tell. And my father's dead." Blair's voice turned cold.

Lana had made a mistake. She had accidentally trod on sensitive territory, but she remembered what else Dr. Walters had said, so apologized quickly.

"I'm sorry. I didn't know. My father is dead, too. But I think he would have wanted me to do what I had to do, really *wanted* to do with my life."

"You're lucky." Blair indicated that talk about fathers was finished. "I'll tell you about my dig in Egypt. I'm eager to get back." Blair went on to describe where she was working, what she hoped to find, what she had already found. Once she got caught up in talking about her work, Blair was so friendly that Lana almost told her about her dreams, almost told her about the magnetic pull that Nefra seemed to have on her. But she was afraid Blair would think she was silly. She admired the woman so much it would be hard to take Blair's laughing at her.

"Lana," Blair stopped abruptly, "Dr. Walters said you thought it was a man who stole the necklace. Do you think it could have been Rodney Newland?"

"Rod?" Lana was shocked. "I don't think so." Apparently, Dr. Walters hadn't shared all he knew with Blair. "Why on earth would he do such a thing?"

"To help Darrah Bey. I knew her parents

in Egypt. I can't see how they had the money to send her over here."

"Maybe there's a fund that pays for exchange students. I think there is." Lana had no idea, but a fund made sense. Probably lots of foreign students had no money to come to the United States. Someone had to sponsor them.

Lana wondered if she should tell Blair that she suspected Antef, and why. But if Antef wasn't guilty, Lana didn't want to jeopardize his job. This was all so confusing. Who to tell what, how much to talk about the theft. How much gossip to start was probably more like it. She really had no provable facts.

"Rod's father was an archaeologist. Rod would know where to sell something like that." Blair was still thinking about Rod being the thief.

"I thought his father worked for the World Health Organization."

"That's his stepfather. His birth father died in an excavation cave-in. Rod was pretty young at the time. The cave-in was close to where archaeologists found Urbena's tomb. Egyptian workers refused to dig any more. They said the accident was caused by Urbena, by her curse."

Why had Rod never told her that? Lana wondered. "You don't believe in that curse — in *any* curse — do you, Blair?"

Blair smiled at Lana. "Stranger things have happened. I find I believe in one thing when I'm here in Denver, but I can start to believe in others when I'm in Egypt. There are forces at work around the tombs that you can't ignore."

Lana glanced at her watch. "I'd better get back. If Marge doesn't get her late afternoon tea, she's grouchy, and I wanted to ask her for a ride home."

"I'll take you," Blair offered.

"Thanks, but Marge lives close. She takes me home all the time. And you'd have to wait till after five."

Blair shrugged and went back for another coffee, leaving her things on their table. Lana waved and hurried back upstairs.

Then, that night, she had the strangest dream of all.

Unable to sleep, I walk in the gardens. The night air is sweet with lotus blossoms. Palm fronds waft gently back and forth in the soft breeze. Nefra's monkey squeals, making me jump. He skitters across my path, chased by another monkey.

Moonlight shines through the row of columns, creating a pattern of light and dark that pleases me.

Tomorrow night I will feel no loneliness. My arms will not be empty, nor cold. I will hold my prince, Nefra, and he will hold me. I will sleep in his arms.

Suddenly the shriek of a falcon rips through the stillness, piercing the air and my heart.

Nefra! What is wrong, my prince?

I feel his pain. I know he reaches out for me and I am not there for him.

Oh, Nefra, Nefra, my love.

Lana sat straight up in bed, the ache inside her unbearable. The pain was so real, as if a poisoned brew had flooded her own chest and pierced her heart.

Looking up, she stopped breathing, her body turning as cold and stiff as any granite that surrounded a king's coffin.

Standing at the foot of her bed was the boy-king, Nefra. His arms reached out to her.

"Urbena, my princess, I have lost you. My love is so great, my longing so unbearable. Come to me. Come and fill my arms with your warmth, your own love. You must return to me or I will continue to die a thousand deaths. I will never sleep until I have you in my arms again."

Chapter 11

The next morning, when Lana woke again, emotion flooded over her until she knew she had to put the dream and the — what happened next — the vision — away for a time or she could not get out of bed. She could not go to school or to work, certainly not back to the museum with her history class field trip.

Taking deep breaths, she forced her mind to go blank, for it to stay that way until she dared look inside again.

Josh was going to have to look at the old stuff in the exhibit whether he wanted to or not. Their history class piled into a yellow bus and drove to the museum on the field trip. Lana tried to join in the party mood, to laugh and tease and anticipate being a tourist. But twice Josh asked her if anything was wrong.

Marge happened to be the lucky volunteer who got the job of leader for the class. "There is a member of your class who knows more than I'll ever know about Egyptology," Marge said, smiling, "but I won't put her on the spot."

Lana felt her face heat up, so Marge might as well have pointed a finger right at her.

Of course, Mr. Drury knew who Marge meant. "She looks as if she stepped right out of Cleopatra's court, too. It's enough to make one believe in reincarnation."

"Yo, Cleo," Josh whispered. "Going to the football game with me tonight?"

"You know I have to work," Lana whispered back.

"I know I'm tired of never seeing you except at school." Josh was serious about what he said, but he was head cheerleader. Lana wouldn't be able to sit with him even if she did go.

"You'll appreciate me more when this is over," she said, "but if you want to take someone else you can." She didn't mean that, but she wanted to give Josh some options. Josh shrugged and stopped at a case full of knives and spearheads.

Lana stopped at the mummy of Nefra and stood beside him while Marge talked. In no time she was surrounded by the warmth she always felt, even though she wasn't alone this time.

"I'm sure you know some of the ritual of preparing a body for burial," Marge said. "The funeral of a common man was probably similar to a funeral today. But when a king died the entire country took part in seventy-two days of mourning. People wept and tore their clothing. They smeared mud on their heads, and walked the streets singing dirges."

"What's a dirge?" Sammy Bittner asked.

"It ain't rock and roll," Mindy Platt said, hanging on his arm, getting the laugh she expected.

"A dirge is a slow, sad piece," Marge answered. "Also, they didn't eat wheat or animal food, or drink wine. They didn't bathe or recline on couches or make love."

"Hey, we would do that for you, Dreary." Sammy used Mr. Drury's nickname. "Wouldn't we class?"

"Yeah, sure, sure we would," most answered.

"For seventy-two days?" Mindy looked doubtful. "That's over two months."

"We'd sure stink." Lucas Murray wrinkled his nose.

Marge wasn't disturbed by all the bantering from the class. "Do you want to hear about making a mummy?"

Everyone did, of course.

"The body was washed and then cut open. The intestines, the heart, the lungs were taken out, washed, and filled with spices. They were smeared with oil and wrapped carefully. You see this jar, the big one. The parts were placed in four alabaster jars. The lids had different figures on top to protect the contents, and the jars were stored with the mummy in the tomb. It was very important to have the intestines preserved intact, for without them a man wouldn't be able to live again."

Sammy had listened as long as he could. "He'd wander through eternity looking for them. Where are my intestines, oh where — "

Even Marge laughed. "I know all of this seems strange to us, but the ceremony was very important to the Egyptian people. Seventy days were spent embalming the body and wrapping it carefully. The coffin makers built at least two coffins, one to fit inside the other. This outer coffin is called a sarcophagus and is usually made of stone. The inner coffin, like you see here for Nefra, was decorated beautifully, and carved with the king's likeness."

Lana looked at Nefra's wooden face. It wasn't hard for her to imagine that he was looking back at her. She remembered her dream and his coming to her last night, and she shivered. Then again, she tried to make her mind a blank and to concentrate on Marge's lecture.

"Is it true that some animals were buried this way, too?" Ann Robbins asked. "I know the Egyptians worshiped cats and other animals. Did they believe the animals would live again?"

"Yes, mummies of cats, crocodiles, hawks, frogs, snakes, scarab beetles, even a scorpion have been found."

"A mummy of a scorpion, ugh!" Josh laughed. "How would you embalm a scorpion?"

Marge ignored the last question. She probably didn't know the answer. "I'm not sure all those animals were worshiped, but they were held sacred. Do you know that in India today cattle and monkeys are sacred?"

"We have sacred animals." Eddie Brooks spoke up. "Mercury Cougars, Jaguars — "

"Says a lot for our culture, doesn't it?" Mr. Drury commented. "Okay, class, we have a short time left. You may go back to any part of the exhibit you want to see again, anything you found particularly fascinating. I'm sure Ms. Wilson will answer any more questions you have, as will I. And Lana, perhaps?" He looked at Lana. "You seem fascinated by this mummy, Lana. Anyone you know? Knew?" he teased.

Wouldn't Mr. Drury be surprised if Lana

answered that she felt as if she knew, had known, Nefra?

"I heard you were here when the wedding necklace was stolen." Mr. Drury was determined to get Lana to talk to him. "Do you think you'll find it?"

"We hope we can." Lana walked away from Nefra, the spell broken. Mr. Drury followed her. "It will certainly be a black mark on our museum if we don't."

"Lana, come over here," Josh called from across the room. Lana smiled at Mr. Drury and walked toward Josh. He took her arm. "Now you owe me one for rescuing you from Dreary."

"Oh, Josh, you're so thoughtful." Lana hugged him. "Listen, I've been thinking. If I ask Marge to take my shift tomorrow night, can we go to a movie?"

Josh pretended he had to think about this unpredictable move on Lana's part. "I'd have to cancel three things, but I think I can manage. Is this the payback for the rescue job?"

"No, maybe you can have an extra hug for that." The idea of a night off pleased Lana. She had been at the museum too much. She realized she was starting to think of nothing except Egypt. "Listen, I'm not going back to school right now, though. Mr. Drury says I can stay here, since classes will be over by the time we get back."

"Okay, I'll call you in the morning." Josh stepped closer and for a second Lana thought he was going to kiss her right in front of Marge, Mr. Drury, and the class, not to mention Antef, who had joined them. Instead Josh whispered in her ear, "I don't really want to take someone else to the game tonight, silly. I'll just have to miss you."

He left her standing there feeling warmth from his love. The rest of the class followed as Drury signaled that it was time to leave. He waved at Lana. "See you tomorrow, Princess."

She wished he hadn't said that. She was starting to suspect that getting her hair cut to deliberately imitate classic Egyptian style was a mistake. But she certainly couldn't feel disappointed that no one had noticed.

She left the exhibit only long enough to freshen up, have a snack, and get her vest.

Marge was at the T-Rex having coffee when Lana hurried in and ordered a Coke. "Lana, come and visit for a minute. You put those kids up to all those questions?"

"Not me. They're creative all by themselves. Don't you wonder how high school teachers survive us year after year?"

"You couldn't pay me enough." Marge laughed. "But then there are a few like you who give us hope."

"Don't put me on a pedestal. Fortunately, I have a lot of interests that keep me out of trouble." Sort of, Lana thought.

"You still having those dreams?"

Lana had finally told Marge about her dreams. She had had to unload on someone, and Marge seemed safe. Now Lana appreciated someone to talk to about what had happened last night. "Marge, last night, I know Nefra came and stood at the foot of my bed. And he called me Urbena. He was so real — so very real. Am I losing it or what?" To her surprise, Lana started to cry.

"You're losing it, honey." Marge moved close and put her arm around Lana. "Maybe you're doing that lucid dreaming stuff where you program your dreams. You want to dream this stuff, so you do."

Lana wondered if there was some truth in what Marge was accusing her of. "Well, I have imagined living in ancient Egypt, and I confess I'm in love with that gorgeous boy-king. But I didn't want to have the dream I had last night or the nightmare I had last week." Lana hadn't told anyone about being buried alive. She related the dream to Marge now.

"My stars. That's enough to keep me awake all night. Wonder why you dreamed that?"

"I have no idea. I — Marge, this is going to sound crazy, but do you believe I could be tapping into — well, into some thoughts or information that's — that's in the air, or in these relics, or — I'm finding it hard to put this into words, but after I had the dream, I wondered if Princess Urbena really did commit suicide or if she could have been murdered."

"You mean you think you dreamed what really happened thousands of years ago? Urbena's mummy isn't here, but Nefra knew what happened, and now he's told you and you dreamed it?"

Lana tried to laugh. "How's that for a plot for a weird movie? Do you think I'm nuts?"

"No, but you're getting really strange, Lana. But hey, you certainly have my attention. I love thinking this could happen. I don't know what good it will do for you to solve a six-thousand-year-old murder mystery."

"I don't either, but — " Lana started to tell Marge that someone today, in the present, was also trying to frighten her. For some reason she didn't. Maybe another time. She wiped her eyes and blew her nose. "Hey, I'd better get to work. We could sit here all night talking, couldn't we? Thanks for being my friend,

Marge. Not many women would want to be-friend a kid with strange ideas."

Marge hugged Lana as they walked out of the T-Rex. "I could hate you because you're beautiful and intelligent and weird, Lana. But I like to think I'm fairly free of prejudice."

"You are, Marge, you are." Lana wondered what Marge would think about Seti, a cat who acted like a dog. She'd tell her that story later. Marge was a good audience.

Sure enough Seti was waiting for Lana out-side the museum when she finished her shift and started home. Lana had stopped worrying and started looking forward to Seti meeting her. The way things were going, this seemed like one of the more normal things that was happening.

They were halfway home when Lana was doubly glad that Seti was with her. She stopped, listened. The night was silent except for passing traffic. A giant harvest moon floated above the horizon and would light up the entire sky in a couple of hours. Lana wished it was light now, or that she'd taken the long way home.

Again she took a few steps. Again she stopped. Footsteps crunched on the gravel be-hind her, but stopped every time she stopped. She got up the nerve to look back every time she stopped, but she couldn't see anyone.

She tried to prepare herself for seeing the mummy figure again. By now she'd thought about it so much, accepted so many strange ideas that had run through her mind, that she wasn't even sure it *was* someone dressed up in a costume. Could it be, was it possible — She glanced over her shoulder, took a few steps, looked back again.

Seti didn't seem alarmed. He ran along just ahead of Lana, and twice he glanced back as if to say, what's wrong? Why aren't you following me?

If — if the mummy, the real mummy of Nefra were following Lana, wouldn't Seti know it? He knew so much. Was she expecting too much of him?

She swung around. "Who is it? Show yourself. I'm not going to be afraid this time. Just come out of the shadows and tell me what you want."

Silence. No insects. No night birds. No couples enjoying the dark pathway.

"Seti. Come." Lana bent down and scooped Seti into her arms. She held the cat close, expecting him to protest. But he didn't. Now he, too, looked back into the shadows. His ears were at full alert. He seemed to be listening.

"Show yourself! I'm not afraid." Lana called out.

This time she got an answer. But not words. Just soft, whispery laughter that went on and on and on. Rising and falling . . . endlessly.

Chapter 12

Lana ran the rest of the way home, not caring if someone was watching, laughing at her. By the time she closed the front door and leaned on it, catching her breath, she felt a knot of anger form in her stomach and icy tremors in her sweaty body.

Seti meowed to let her know she was still clutching him tightly. He hadn't complained once about bumping along in her arms as she ran.

"What can I do, Seti, what can I do?" she whispered as she set him on the floor.

"What can you do about what?" She didn't realize her mother was standing close enough to hear her.

"Oh, nothing, Mom. Nothing. I have so much to do to keep up with school and this job. It's worth it, though, so don't think I'm complaining. Just trying to decide what to do first."

"Lana, you've always worked harder for what you want than any kid I know. I'm proud of you. Do you know that? I hardly ever remember to say it." Her mother pulled her close and hugged her. Lana hugged back, enjoying becoming a little girl and having her mother comfort her.

"Thanks, Mom. I have a good role model. You worked really hard after Dad died to keep things together, to buy this house. I love you."

"I love you, too, Sweetie. Hungry?"

"Of course. What's for dinner?" Lana wasn't sure she could choke down any food, but when she smelled the vegetarian pizza that was one of her mother's tastiest concoctions, she changed her mind. She pushed away the whispering—her fear, her anger. She washed her hands at the kitchen sink, sank into a chair, and let her mother wait on her.

"Why don't you take one of the new mysteries I brought home from the library, go to bed early, and read?" Mrs. Richardson had watched Lana eat and now sat at the table with her, drinking a cup of coffee. "Take your mind entirely off Egypt. Scare yourself while safely in your bed."

Lana had enough of a mystery on her hands without taking on someone else's plot. And she certainly didn't need to scare herself further. But maybe it would be distracting. And the safety of her bed sounded wonderful.

Seti was perfectly willing to go to bed early. He curled into the folds of the fluffy comforter that Lana pulled up almost to her chin. For a few minutes he purred, then he slept so deeply he stopped making any sound.

About nine-thirty, when the main character in Lana's book had gone into an old house by herself — silly woman — Seti woke and leaped off the bed. He jumped onto the windowsill and stared out into the darkness.

"See anything?" Lana asked.

Meow, Seti replied. Then he wiped at the window pane with his paw. *Meow*.

"I was going to keep that window closed, Seti. Not that it does any good. You'd find a way to get out.

Seti blinked and patted the window again.

"You have a box downstairs."

Seti patted the window a third time.

"Oh, all right. But come back in two shakes of a cat's tail." Lana got out of her warm nest and raised the window slightly, then pushed the screen out, leaving a narrow crack. She'd close it when he came back. He never strayed far from her anytime she was home. It was almost as if he were guarding her. She laughed at the idea. Guarded by royalty, a sacred black cat.

Her eyes returned to the book, and she read until the page began to blur. She struggled to keep her lids open. They got heavier and heavier. Automatically, one hand raised slowly, snapped off the bed lamp, and she slid down into the soft warmth of a dream.

I walk in a procession, tall, proud, wearing a heavy headpiece and a long gown with a train dragging the ground. In my hand I carry a staff like a scepter. On one side of me a slave carries a polished wooden stand, holding Nefra's favorite book. On the other side another slave bears Nefra's hunting hawk, tethered to his wrist. On a small wooden platform, carried by a third slave, rides a cat. It is Seti sitting tall, regal. His tail curls round his body and across his front feet. He stares straight ahead, his expression solemn.

The air is sweet-smelling from the perfume of many bouquets of flowers, but the sweetness contrasts with wailing and moaning, screeching, and crying. I look down and find my dress, although new, is ripped and frayed as if I have torn it myself in my agony.

*My heart is a heavy granite stone. My white
slippers shuffle slowly through the dust, soiled
and ruined, moving to the beat of the mournful
music.*

*I feel tears slide down my cheeks, amazed
there are any left to shed now that this day has
arrived.*

*Despite the cacophony of sounds around me,
I hear the tiny, intrusive noise.*

A thin, papery rattle slipped into Lana's consciousness. Slowly she came awake and realized she was in her bedroom, not in some
— some procession.

Again she heard the skittering noise as if
Seti was knocking a ball of paper across her
bedroom floor.

"Seti? Is that you?" She reached up and
flicked on the bedside lamp. "Seti?" She
glanced at the window, realizing she hadn't
closed it when Seti came back. That she had
fallen asleep before Seti returned. Had he
come back?

She pulled herself upright. "Seti, where are
you?"

Just as she was about to throw back the
covers and step out onto the cold floor, she
heard the skitter again. The sound was like a
hoarse whisper along the floor.

Leaning slightly, her eyes traveled past the braided rug beside the bed and into the shadow near the rocker three feet away. Her left hand tightened on the roll of comforter in her fist. Her right hand tried to dig into the mattress at her side.

Crawling across the floor were two huge scorpions, side by side as if partners in some bizarre ballet. They slid along together, tails curled overhead, ready to use their painful weapons.

Her right hand flew to her mouth, stifling the scream that lodged behind her clenched teeth.

The scream escaped and shredded the night air as she spotted the third scorpion, poised three inches from her left hand, in the bed with her.

Chapter 13

Lana, holding herself perfectly still, screamed at her mother who rushed into the room. "Be careful! On the floor."

"What? Oh, my lord, where did those come from?" Her mother turned on the overhead light so she could see better.

Lana didn't want her mother, who was barefoot, to walk across her room. But she had to get rid of the scorpion on her bed. She took a deep breath, gripped the coverlet tighter, and flipped the scorpion onto the floor. "Did you see where it went? Keep an eye on it."

"Close to the others. I'll be right back. I'm getting the broom."

Lana stared at the three scorpions, now fighting each other. When her mother returned, Lana put on her slippers and carefully got out of bed, looking for more scorpions with every step.

"I'll hold this dustpan, Lana. You sweep them into it." Her mother had taken time to slip into her shoes and now circled the scorpions. One was skittering off toward the closet.

"Don't let it get in there." Lana brushed one scorpion into the dustpan her mother held. "What are you going to do with it?"

"There's only one place that's sure." Her mother hurried out of the room, then Lana heard a flush. Down the toilet.

The other two, still dancing around each other, tails arched high, went into the pan together and were swiftly flushed down the toilet.

Lana still didn't trust that there were only three scorpions. She and her mother searched the room thoroughly before they decided they'd found them all. That's when Lana found the note. She wadded it into her hand as Mrs. Richardson collapsed on Lana's bed.

"What — where in the world did those come from? I've never seen a scorpion in this house before. And surely not three at once and in the fall."

Glancing at the window, Lana saw that the screen was open wider than before. Seti chose that moment to step back inside.

"Where were you when I needed you?"

Lana scolded, but in a way she was glad Seti hadn't been there. He probably would have been stung. He bounced onto her bed. Lana gathered him into her arms and hugged him tight.

"He was outside?"

"I think someone pushed the scorpions through the window, Mom. Sorry, I opened it for Seti. He wanted out badly."

Lana's mother shook her head. "But why would someone do anything like that?"

Lana sighed. She was going to have to tell her mother a little of what was going on. She chose that moment to read the note. "I found this note on the floor." She smoothed the crinkled paper and read.

ADMIT YOU ARE THE PRINCESS.
I WOULDN'T WANT TO MAKE A MISTAKE.
NEFRA

The signature was false, of course, and the message was printed in block letters that anyone could have written.

"Does that make any sense to you, Lana?" Her mother took the note and stared at it.

"Someone has been — has been teasing me, Mom. Pulling tricks on me. Trying to frighten me, I guess."

"But why?" Her mother was stuck on that word. If Lana knew why, she might also know who.

"I have no idea. The first incident was when the lights went off at the museum and someone whispered to me, trying to frighten me."

Lana told her mother most of what had been happening. She didn't mention that she was followed and someone in a mummy suit had frightened her in the park. She had such a fear of being grounded, her mother refusing to let her go anyplace, losing her freedom. Her mother would want to drive her everywhere, pick her up, know where she was at every minute.

"Maybe it has something to do with stealing the necklace. Whoever — " Her mother ran her hand over Seti's fur. Seti looked at her and meowed.

"I heard the whispering voice the very night the exhibit opened. Before the necklace was stolen."

"What does this mean, admit you are the princess?"

"People have been teasing me about looking like the princess Urbena. You know, she was supposed to marry Nefra. Someone has taken the teasing a step further."

Her mother kept staring at the note. She

had no more thoughts on the matter than Lana did, if as many.

Suddenly Lana felt totally exhausted. "Mom, I've got to get some sleep. We can talk tomorrow. I don't want you to worry."

"I'm *going* to worry. You can't stop me." Her mother stood up, walked over, and closed Lana's window, locking it firmly. "Someone climbed this tree." She stared out into the darkness.

"It's an easy tree to climb, and they didn't have to go high." Lana shook the covers of her bed and remade it. She slipped under the covers, her eyes heavy, the adrenaline rush long gone, leaving her more exhausted than ever.

"Are you going to be all right?" Mrs. Richardson snapped off the overhead light and stood in the doorway to the bedroom.

"Yes, Mom. Thanks." Lana reached for the lamp switch. She was just too tired to lie awake afraid.

Lana took the note with her to the museum the next day, stuck it in her pocket to look at again, as if it would finally make sense.

She had the early shift, and was surprised to find Rod Newland waiting for her at the door. "I have permission to sketch some of the artifacts, today, Lana. I did that in Cairo. I have a whole notebook full of sketches." He was going to show them to her, but she stopped him. Somehow she wasn't in the mood.

"Where's Antef? He was supposed to open up. I don't have a key."

"I haven't seen him." Rod closed the notebook, obviously disappointed that Lana didn't seem excited about his work.

She wasn't totally out of touch. "I'll look at them later, Rob. Let's try again to have lunch together. We have to open now. People will be in line here in no time." She glanced down the hall. "I'll go get another key."

She hurried to the museum office, but happened across one of the custodians on the way downstairs. "Mr. Lowman, can you open the exhibit for me? Antef Raam was supposed to be here, but I don't see him and the door is locked."

"Sure, Lana." The elderly man followed Lana back up the escalator, which had yet to be turned on. "There'll be a huge crowd today."

"I know. That's why we have to get ready. Thank goodness I came early." Lana was at least forty-five minutes early, so early no other volunteers had arrived, nor had all of the employees. She had planned to look at the entire exhibit carefully, to make sure that everything was in place.

She was becoming paranoid about anything having to do with the show. Maybe what was happening was some elaborate scheme to steal some other artifacts. Annoying her — well, frightening her — was just an extra part of their game. Someone was entertaining himself at her expense but at the same time planning to steal the relics.

Did this have something to do with her deliberately trying to look like an ancient Egyptian? She had thought it would be fun. She was so taken with the exhibit coming, with the whole life of these ancient peoples. Had she gone way too far in identifying with them? Someone had noticed her immediately. Be truthful, Lana, she said to herself, *everyone* noticed you immediately. But one person thought that making her a part of his game was irresistible.

Was it Rod? She remembered Blair's question, her suspicion. Rod and Darrah together? Did they need money that badly? Rod acted so innocent, but maybe he had the ability to do that. Or he was another person around Darrah. She knew girls with that kind of power. They could talk a guy into doing anything.

Mr. Lowman got the door opened and propped back. Lana darted inside, flipping on the lights, looking from case to case, display to display, fully expecting something to be out of place, something to be missing. The first room was exactly as it had been from the night the exhibit had opened.

"You okay?" Rod had noticed her nervousness.

"Sure. I guess I was spooked because Antef wasn't here and we had to open. Put your stool down anyplace, and we'll stumble over you all morning." She teased Rod, but gave him a big smile to make up for it. Maybe she should tell him some of what had been happening over lunch, and watch his reaction. She wouldn't mind unloading on someone else. Her mother didn't count, since she was too distanced from the museum and the people working here. Would Josh be sympathetic? He'd care, but he might just laugh at her fear.

At first glance, the second room of the exhibit looked all right, too. The case that had replaced the one holding the wedding necklace looked awfully bare. Dr. Walters had deliberately left the top shelf vacant to receive the necklace once they found it. He wanted the public aware of what had happened, and to have everyone in Denver looking for the jeweled collar.

Nefra lay just as he'd been for two weeks. Lana was almost getting used to the warmth she stepped into as she walked to the coffin. The aura was exactly like a force field that closed around her, making her feel euphoric. But she couldn't stay here long today. She had work to do.

Before she fell under the mummy's spell, she heard a scratching sound and a muffled thud.

She looked at Nefra's beautiful green basalt sarcophagus, standing beside his coffin. No, not from there. Urbena's coffin lay prone nearby. It was supposed to be open.

The case was closed, the lid resting tightly on the ornately-painted coffin. The scratching noise was coming from Urbena's coffin. Someone — or something — was closed up inside!

Chapter 14

For a few seconds Lana froze in place. Her hand gripped the side of Nefra's coffin so tightly that her knuckles turned white.

"Be sensible," she whispered. "The lid has simply been moved."

"Rod! Rod! Come in here." Lana ran toward the other room while she yelled.

Marge appeared before Rod could answer. "Lana, what's wrong?"

"Rod, get Rod." Lana didn't know why she thought she needed Rod. She and Marge could probably lift the lid. But because she'd thought of him first, she wanted him, too.

He hurried into the room. "What's the matter, Lana?"

"The coffin — Urbena's coffin — someone's inside." Words sputtered from Lana's lips. She couldn't put a complete sentence together.

"Someone is in that coffin?" Marge asked, staring.

They all heard the scratching and thumping and for seconds looked at each other with unasked questions.

"Hurry." Rod took hold at the foot of the coffin lid.

Lana and Marge took the sides near the top. The three of them lifted the heavy lid, slid it off, and set it on the floor.

Lana stared inside. Slowly Antef sat up, looking dazed. Then he started to cough as if his lungs were coated with thousand-year-old dust.

"I'll get some water," Marge said, hurrying away.

"How long have you been in there?" Lana asked.

"I came over early to — to — " Antef bent over with a coughing spell. "Early — I — early — someone — too early." Gratefully, he took the paper cup of water Marge handed him and sipped.

Lana was having trouble being patient. "Someone put you in there?" Silly. He didn't get in the coffin himself.

"Someone hit me. That's the last I remember until I woke up in here."

"You must have been terrified." Rod

frowned. "Why would someone do this?"

Lana stared at Rod. He came to the museum early. How early? As early as Antef? But why would he do this to Antef? Why would anyone, for that matter?

Antef looked pale and frightened. "Is anything missing? Maybe something was stolen. Maybe I let in a thief."

"I've already looked at everything in the other room. I had almost finished looking over this one. I don't think anything is gone but the necklace." Lana moved to look at the other cases. She came back as Marge and Rod were helping Antef out of the coffin.

Antef patted his pockets as if to see if he personally had been robbed. The right-hand pocket of his vest crackled as if stuffed with paper. Momentarily his hand stopped there, then he looked at Lana. "Thank you. Thank you for finding me."

"Visitors are starting to come in, Antef." Lana noticed the curious look on the face of a couple who stepped into the second room. To find three people standing around the coffin of Urbena — or had they seen them help Antef out? — they had to wonder what games the staff had been playing.

"I think you'd better see if Dr. Walters is here. If he is, tell him what happened. You could have been seriously hurt," Lana said, now worried about Antef.

Antef hurried away, and Lana prepared to guide the first group through the exhibit. Instead of standing in one place today, she was helping Marge lead tours. She struggled to put her mind on what she needed to say.

"You think it's all right for me to stay and sketch?" Rod asked her.

"Of course. Why not? Don't forget you're going to show me your sketchbook at lunch." Lana wanted time to ask Rod some questions. She couldn't say, "Did you put Antef in that coffin?" But maybe she could ask questions about what time he arrived this morning and see if he appeared to be telling the truth.

The possibility that Rod might be playing tricks on her or anyone at the museum would never have occurred to Lana if Blair hadn't brought up his name. Now his involvement was uppermost in her mind. While she led the tours automatically, she quickly made a list of possible suspects. But at first, she couldn't think of anyone. She had been so busy wondering *why*, she'd forgotten to wonder *who*.

After guiding two groups through the exhibit, Lana decided she was close enough to break time to stop for a few minutes. She felt as if she'd never had time to recover from the shock of finding Antef in the coffin before she'd had to go to work.

Then she saw Antef himself returning to work. He glanced around, not seeing her approaching, patted his pocket again, then took out a wadded piece of paper and smoothed it.

"What does your note say?" Lana stood beside him, and what she saw shocked her.

Antef jumped with surprise. He stuffed the paper back into his vest pocket and tried to pretend it was nothing. "Nothing, it's nothing. A list of things I meant to do."

"In block letters signed by Nefra?" She'd been close enough to see the letters. She guessed the rest.

Antef's face paled. His eyes widened. He stepped back again from Lana, as if *she* frightened him.

"Have a cup of coffee with me, Antef."

"I — I — " Antef looked confused and even more frightened. Lana felt she was looking at a small child instead of a grown man.

She took his arm. "I think you need strong coffee with all that sugar in it that you like."

Antef let Lana lead him to the T-Rex cafe. She sat him at the farthest table to the back of the hall and went to get two coffees. When she returned he was slumped in his chair, looking dazed and confused. He hadn't recovered from the shock of the morning, either, she suspected.

"Did you talk to Dr. Walters?" Lana set Antef's coffee before him, and tore and emptied two little packets of sugar into it. She stirred it for him. He didn't seem capable of doing even the simplest act.

"He is coming in by eleven." Antef did manage to look at his watch. Then he sipped the coffee little by little until it was gone. Color returned to his cheeks, and his skin, once a yellowish-tan, was coming back to mahogany.

Lana gave him time, even though she was anxious to see his note and compare the printing to hers. If the same person wrote both, maybe together they could guess who it was.

"Antef, last night someone dumped three scorpions into my bedroom. A note came with them." Lana reached in her pocket and took out the three-by-five piece of paper, smoothed it, and handed it to Antef.

He studied it without giving Lana his note. "What does it mean?"

"I have no idea, Antef. But someone has been trying to frighten me. What have you done to make someone knock you out and put you in that coffin? What does your note say?"

Reluctantly, it would seem, Antef spread out his paper and handed it to Lana.

RETURN MY NECKLACE.
IT BELONGS TO MY PRINCESS.
THIS IS YOUR ONLY WARNING.
NEFRA

"Someone thinks you took the jeweled collar, Antef," Lana said, looking at the note. *"Did you?"* She stared at him.

"I — I know nothing of this." Antef didn't look at Lana as he spoke. "Why would I steal from my government?"

"I don't know." Lana kept looking at him. "I ripped the button off your vest that night, someone attacked me, Antef. I smelled your aftershave. I know it was you, Antef. You might as well admit it."

"I know nothing." Antef reached out and smoothed the note that had been placed in the coffin with him. "I must meet Dr. Walters. I will tell him there is a crazy person trying to make trouble." Antef left quickly, without looking at her. He was certainly hiding something. If not the necklace, what?

Lana watched him go, finishing her own cup of coffee, waiting for the caffeine jolt she needed to go back and pretend nothing was out of the ordinary at the museum.

She looked at the list of people she had written down this morning. For lack of a better idea, she had listed everyone at the museum, everyone who had anything to do with the exhibit at all. Even Dr. Walters. Even Blair Vaughn, and Antef, and Rod. She had put Antef at the top of the list, even though it would have been difficult for him to seal himself inside that coffin. But he was feeling terribly guilty about something. And he was hiding something from her.

She got out the stub of pencil she kept in her pocket. She scratched Marge Wilson off the list. Marge was the sanest person she knew. And maybe the only one she could trust. Should she tell her everything she knew? Get Marge to help her figure out who was trying to cause trouble? Before someone got hurt?

She'd wait until she had lunch with Rod to make a decision.

Chapter 15

"Who do you think put Antef in that coffin?" Rod asked as he and Lana headed for lunch at the T-Rex.

"I was thinking maybe you did," Lana answered, flippant, tossing off the remark like a joke, wanting to see Rod's reaction.

"That's what I like about you, Lana. You have a great sense of humor. Now why would I lock up Antef like a mummy?"

"I don't know. I was going to ask you why. He was there early. You were there early."

"I wasn't there that early. You think it has something to do with the necklace disappearing, that the two are connected?"

"Maybe. Someone might be trying to frighten him into returning it."

"Why not just tell the police he took it?"

"Because I'm not sure. I only suspect Antef." Lana got in line and ordered a tuna sandwich and a Coke.

Rod insisted on buying her lunch. "This is a business lunch. I want your opinion on my sketches, Lana. I value your judgment. Several people have encouraged me to go to art school, but I really want to combine art and archaeology."

Lana didn't know why Rod valued her opinion so much. And she felt a little guilty. Here she was meeting with Rod to try to decide if he was behind the mysteries at the museum, and he was flattering her, asking for her opinion on what to do with the rest of his life. She relaxed a little, but she didn't cross him off her list. He might just be a good actor.

They found a table and sat down. He smiled at her, his brown eyes warm, also flattering her. *Please don't be guilty, please don't be causing all this trouble, Rod.* She could like this guy. She could like him a lot. He gave her shivers that she had never experienced with Josh. And she and Rod had so many interests in common.

"Where are you going to school?" That was a safe thing to ask. "I guess I'll go to CU Boulder. I've applied there."

"I haven't decided. Dad wants me to go to Cambridge."

"In England?" Lana could forget seeing Rod at college. "Your real father or your step-father?"

Rod stared at her. Finally he looked away. "My birth father was an archaeologist. He died in an excavation in Egypt when I was two. My mother remarried when I was still very young. My stepfather is the only father I know. We're close. He may go back to Cairo, so it won't matter where I live. I'm feeling kind of mixed-up about college right now."

Lana kept quiet for a few minutes and nibbled her sandwich. If Rod wanted to talk, she'd listen. But he started to eat, too, and flipped through the pages of his sketchbook.

"Here's one of my better sketches." He pushed the open book toward her.

She swung it around and studied the pencil sketch. Not only was it accurate and well drawn, but something about it made it leap right off the page. She wanted to touch the funeral jar, smooth her hands over the figures on the lid.

"Rod." She realized her voice was full of awe. "This is better than good. This is wonderful! The jar is so real, but better than a photograph."

"You're not just saying that?" Rod's lack of confidence made Lana see him in a different light. She'd thought he was a bit conceited and hard to approach. Had he been covering a lack of faith in himself despite his experience and talent?

"My father says there's no money in art or archaeology. He wants me to go into business administration. My mother says my real father was a dreamer and never would have made enough money to send me through college. So I'd better be grateful that there's money and I'd better take advantage of it." Rod's voice took on some anger and bitterness. Lana reached out and took his hand.

"He's probably right, Rod, but I've always thought a person should follow his heart. I'm going to do what I want to do. I always have." She smiled, remembering. "I had an eighth-grade English teacher who tried to convince me I was too obsessed by one subject — Egypt. I wrote all my papers about Egypt. All my essays, all my stories, were set in Egypt. She said it wasn't healthy for someone my age to have only one interest. She even tried to assign me different subject matter."

Rod smiled. "So what did you do then?"

"I wrote what I wanted to anyway and dared her to flunk me. She knew she couldn't. Finally she gave up and started pestering another student. I'm going to be an archaeologist, no matter what anyone says. After I graduate from college, I'll try to have faith that I'll get a job — in Egypt, of course." She smiled back at him and made a decision. "Rod, can I ask you what you think about something else? I think it's related to my obsession. I've been having the strangest dreams."

"Dreams? What kind of dreams?"

She paged through his sketchbook for a minute before she spoke. Rod's drawings were special. He had incredible talent. She could feel him watching her, waiting.

"You have to do something with your art, Rod. You'll let yourself down if you don't."

"What kind of dreams?" he insisted, ready to pay attention to her. To focus attention away from his own problems.

"I dream I'm back in ancient Egypt. Most of the time the dream is about everyday life. The other night I found myself in a funeral procession, but that was probably influenced by our field trip and Marge telling us about funerals."

"Who are you in the dream?"

"This is going to sound silly."

"Sometimes dreams *are* silly."

"In the funeral, I think I was Princess Urbena. I was in the funeral procession for Nefra. Rod, it was so real. I felt the terrible sadness, the loss."

"Have you always dreamed a lot, vividly?"

"Not like this. These dreams are so real. I've steeped myself in Egyptology for months, so the subject matter is inevitable, but not the feelings. I've never had dreams with these kinds of feelings, and I wake up retaining the sorrow, the joy, or once, the fear."

"The fear?"

She took a deep breath. She might as well tell Rod about her nightmare.

"I think I was the princess in that dream. I was knocked out, placed in a coffin, and buried alive. I woke up feeling suffocated, and really scared. The dream made me wonder if the princess did commit suicide or if she was murdered."

"You know, Lana, because I spent so much time in Egypt I believe in some things I wouldn't otherwise, like the supernatural. I think you can tap into the consciousness of someone in another time, another place. I think the brain has powers we haven't even begun to realize."

"You think because I've been thinking about Urbena a lot, I could have — have made contact with her? That in a dream she could show me what happened to her?"

"I also believe in reincarnation. You could have been Urbena in another life."

Lana was overwhelmed . . . frightened. "I can't believe that. Anyway, wouldn't she have come back in Egypt?"

"I don't think souls have any geographical boundaries. I know a woman here in Denver who says she shares a soul with a man in India."

"But in order to share a soul, you have to be on earth at the same time." Lana thought about that a little. She tried to stay open to any idea. "But back to my being Urbena. You think I might be remembering what happened to me in another life?"

"Sounds spooky, doesn't it?" Rod took her hand. "There's no way you could ever prove it, but I find it fascinating to think about. The entire history of the rulers of Egypt is full of murder, jealousy, people claiming the throne. So Urbena, even though she held no claim to the crown, could have been murdered for some other reason."

"Well, what a cozy little lunchtime." A voice, a hard, angry voice, interrupted their conversation. It was Darrah. Her dark eyes shot daggers at Lana.

Rod let go of Lana's hand and grasped his sandwich tightly. "Hi, Darrah. I didn't know you were coming over."

"Obviously you didn't." Darrah glared at Lana. Lana had never seen such open hatred and jealousy. "I thought I'd surprise you and we could go to lunch together. I made a mistake. I'm sorry." She spun around on one foot, marched around the corner, and out of the museum.

Rod stared after her. Finally he said, "I met her in Cairo. We've been friends for a long time. She's always been jealous."

"I guess so. Sorry if I ruined your love life." Lana was only halfway teasing.

"Not your fault. Not your problem. I guess I'd better talk to Darrah. I think she came to Denver because of me, and — but — "

"You don't have to explain." Lana ate the last of her sandwich. "I'd better get back to work."

"Lana, thanks for saying my work was good. That means a lot to me. I haven't shown it to many people."

"Then I'm flattered. Thank you."

"Would you go out with me some time?" Rod studied her, totally serious.

"I don't know. I'm going with Josh Benson and you — "

"Yeah, I have some fences to mend, and an understanding to reach, but after that?"

"I might consider it. Ask me again. After the exhibit is over I'll have more time."

"That won't be long." Rod got up to follow Darrah, if he could find her. Maybe she did this a lot, blowing up. Maybe it was a game and she'd be waiting for him outside. Their relationship was none of Lana's business, but she was curious. It would seem that Darrah thought Rod was her property, but Rod had a different opinion.

"I never thought I'd say it, but I think I'll be glad when the exhibit is over. A lot of strange things have been happening in the last two weeks. Good luck with Darrah." She smiled at Rod.

"Thanks." He grinned. "I may need it. If Darrah were an Egyptian queen, my head would be under the ax by now."

He waved and headed for the front door. Lana walked slowly to the bathroom before she returned to the exhibit.

Just inside the door someone grabbed her arm. Darrah's face was a mask of pure anger, robbing her of all her beauty.

"Leave Rod alone, Lana. He's mine, all mine. I'm warning you just this once."

Lana pried Darrah's fingers off her arm.

"And what will you do if I don't? You don't own Rod." Lana felt perverse and angry, too. Darrah had no right to speak to her this way. To tell her she couldn't be friends with Rod.

"The ancients aren't the only ones who can place a curse on a person. I'll make sure you regret not obeying me. You act like some kind of princess who owns this place, but you don't own Rod. I do. I'll make you regret you ever met him or me. I'll get you when you're least expecting it."

Lana couldn't walk away. "Don't threaten me!" Darrah's tirade brought out a side of Lana she didn't like, but she refused to back down.

"Try me!" Darrah whirled and dashed out of the bathroom. Lana was left to cool off her own anger with cold water over her face and hands.

"You do seem to be upsetting a number of people all of a sudden, Princess." Lana spoke to her image in the mirror. She stared at the face — one that seemed as if it belonged to someone else, to another time, another place. Finally it relaxed into a smile — a half smile. Not much was funny today.

Upstairs a group was waiting for her. She pushed Darrah out of her mind, but continued to think about what Rod had said about being Urbena. She felt so at home among the artifacts, and she loved entertaining the visitors with stories about Nefra and Urbena and about other kings and queens.

"You look like this princess yourself," one man commented, pointing to Urbena's coffin. It was a remark Lana had heard so often she was starting to believe it.

I may be, she thought, letting the strange idea take hold of her. I may be this Egyptian princess. If I am, that would explain this pull that Nefra has on me.

She smiled at the man, entered the warm presence of the boy-king, and began to tell his story.

Chapter 16

Seti didn't meet her after work that day, and she was relieved that he'd stopped playing his game of caretaker and personal bodyguard. When she got home, however, she looked all over the house — which didn't take long, since their house was small.

"Seti," she called. He knew his name. "Seti, where are you? Seti, come." She even whistled, knowing cats heard high, sharp sounds easily.

Her bedroom window was closed and locked. Mom had made sure of that last night, and Lana had checked it again before she left for the museum this morning.

"Seti. Seti!" She held back her panic, opening closet doors, then starting on dresser drawers. Surely he'd meow if he was trapped someplace.

In the kitchen she opened all the cupboards,

the pantry, then searched the small storage area off the kitchen by the back door. This was their "mess room," her mother had said. Everyone had to have one room or part of a room for making a mess, piling recycling things — newspapers, aluminum cans, bottles.

When she was absolutely certain that Seti wasn't in the house, she called her mother, who'd had to work again today. The department store was having a big November sale and needed all the help they could bring in to get ready for it.

"Mom, did you see Seti before you left for work?"

"No, I don't remember seeing him. Isn't he home?"

"I can't find him anyplace in the house." Lana was close to tears. "Do you think he slipped out when you left? He's good at that."

"Calm down, Lana." Her mother's voice was soothing. "Remember that Seti came to us. He was a stray, I assume. So he's very independent, and able to take care of himself."

"I wish I could believe that."

"Retrace your route to the museum. Maybe he set out to meet you and — and got distracted."

Lana filled in what her mother didn't want to say. Got hit by a car. Chased by a dog. She didn't think she needed to add picked up by some kids bent on mischief. Seti seemed pretty good at defending himself — and her. She couldn't help but remember the night he'd chased away the mummy — whoever that was who was trying to frighten her.

Putting on a heavier coat with a hood, she stepped back outside. The wind was blowing ahead of a storm, a cold wind. Clouds rolled and tumbled in the west, over the mountains. Surely if Seti could get home, he would have come. Animals know when bad weather is coming. He wouldn't want to be caught outside in the first real snowstorm of the season.

Ducking her head and turning her back to the wind, she let it push her down the sidewalk toward the museum. She half walked, half stumbled all the way to the park and then the grounds outside the huge building.

"Seti," she called over and over. "Seti, come."

Gusts of wind swept her voice away. She yelled louder. She stopped several people asking them if they'd seen a black cat. When she turned and headed back home, the wind punished her cheeks and snatched her words almost before she could open her mouth. She tugged the hood close to her ears, which had started to ache.

Instead of yelling more she started to concentrate on Seti, getting an image of him in her mind. She begged him to hear her, to know she needed him, to come back to her. If he was lost and felt the connection, he'd know which way to run. He'd know to come to her.

Returning to her neighborhood, she knocked on every door, asking about Seti. It didn't matter if she knew the people or not, and she didn't know too many of the neighbors. Many houses were rentals, many were bought and sold often. The area changed so often that neither she nor her mother bothered to get acquainted. They were both busy and had friends away from home.

Striking out, she at least had the satisfaction of knowing if anyone living close saw Seti — found him — his body — they'd call her.

But deep in her heart, she knew Seti wasn't dead. The connection was still there for her, and she was sure she'd know if Seti was hurt or — or worse.

Despite that knowledge, she felt a weight in her chest, around her heart, as if the wind had reached inside and iced her lungs, slowed the blood pumping in and out of her heart. She felt sluggish and unable to breathe.

Her mother had gotten home. She rushed

to the front door when Lana opened it. "Lana, did you find him?"

Lana shook her head, unable to speak. Her mother took her coat and threw it on the porch, put one arm around Lana and pulled her into the kitchen.

"I made a pot of hot, strong tea. I hoped you'd be home soon. Look at you, you're frozen."

Lana cupped both hands around the mug of amber liquid that her mother placed in front of her at the kitchen table. She sipped until a small chunk of the ice inside her melted.

"I can't bear it if anything has happened to him, Mom. I never got close to a cat this fast."

"Now, Lana, nothing has happened to Seti. I feel that. I'm sure of it, and I don't even know why."

"I feel the same way, but it doesn't help much when I can't hold him in my lap."

Lana's body grew tired, exhausted. She ate a few bites of the stew her mother warmed for them, but it seemed to stick in her throat and create a huge ache. The ache grew larger until her entire chest hurt. If she breathed deeply, stabs of pain almost made her cry out. When she crawled into bed, she lay there whimpering. She stuffed the pillow around her face so her mother wouldn't hear her.

Her mother liked cats, too, but Lana was afraid she'd scold her for taking on so over a cat. A cat who had come to them and only stayed a couple of weeks. He wasn't like Muffy who had been a part of the family for so long.

But Seti was family. That was what was strange when Lana thought about it. She had fallen in love with Seti the minute she set eyes on him. At first purr.

"Seti, oh, Seti, please come back."

She slipped out of bed and opened the window a crack, pushed the screen away from the sill just enough for a slender cat to slip through.

Cold wind whistled through the narrow opening. She didn't care. It didn't matter how cold she got. Outside someplace, Seti was colder.

She threw the afghan her mother had knitted over her puffy comforter, slid back into bed, and huddled there until she started to get warm again.

She didn't know when she fell asleep, or how long she had slept. She only knew something woke her. What woke her wasn't a dream. Her mind was dark, like a movie theater after hours.

No, what woke her was a thump. A bumping sound like Seti had jumped from the window to the floor.

Sitting up, she snapped on the light. "Seti? Is that you?" She patted the bed. "I knew you were alive. Come here, you must be frozen."

No shivering cat appeared, and there was no tiny meow saying thank goodness I found my way home.

But the wind wailed louder through the open window, and a plinking noise suggested that rain or sleet was hitting the screen. The storm had arrived.

She pushed back the covers, feeling the cold air whip right through her nightgown. Her feet touched the icy floor, and, remembering the scorpions, she glanced around before she walked farther.

The cold didn't stop at her skin, but seeped inside, quickly chilling her all the way through. A different kind of cold started in her stomach and zipped up her windpipe into her throat. Something was wrong. Seti hadn't jumped in the window. *Something else had.*

She rushed to the light switch by her door, flipped it on so she could see better. Only then did she dare look at the floor beside the window.

When she did, when her eyes focused, she started to scream.

Wrapped in gauze, a perfect mummy of a cat sat upright.

Chapter 17

Lana's screams had progressed to hysteria by the time her mother reached her.

"Lana, Lana, what's wrong?" Her mother flew into the room and wrapped her arms around Lana, trying to calm her. She held Lana tight and patted her back. "What's wrong, honey?"

When Lana got a little control, she pointed to the object on the floor below her window, staring at it again herself.

"Seti," Lana sobbed. "Seti." That was all she could say.

"Oh, no." Her mother breathed out the words softly. "It can't be. Who would do such a thing?" Then anger filled her voice. "I'm calling the police this time, Lana. They would have laughed if I'd have called and said someone put scorpions in my daughter's room, but this is different."

Mrs. Richardson pulled Lana along with her to use the phone in the kitchen. She pressed Lana into a hard-backed chair while she dialed 911.

A patrol car was in the neighborhood. Two uniformed men were at the door within two minutes.

"You stay here, Lana," her mother suggested and led the officers to Lana's bedroom.

Something inside Lana would not let her sit there in the kitchen while strangers tended to Seti. She followed them.

Both officers stared at the cat mummy for a few seconds as if they couldn't believe what they were seeing.

"You think this is your cat?" the short, blond one said.

"Isn't it obvious?" Lana's mother was getting angry. Lana heard the control in her voice.

The man looked at his partner and shrugged. Then he walked over and picked up the gauze-wrapped figure. He stared at it, then started to unwind the bandages. He peeled off the gauze slowly as if he himself didn't want to see what was underneath.

Lana held her fist to her mouth, pressing in another spate of hysterical screams. Why was she watching? She couldn't *not* watch. As bad as this was, she had to see it. She had to know.

Black fur started to show as the last layer fell away into a long, gray spiral piling up at the police officer's feet. When the last of the gauze spilled to the floor, he continued to stare at the object in his hand.

Lana ran to him and grabbed the cat from him. A stuffed toy! Not Seti. Not her cat. But a child's toy.

Tears of relief ran down her face in tiny rivers. Once more she broke into hysterical crying, this time from relief.

"It's not Seti. It's not! It's not!" She sobbed until she had all the anguish out of her system. No one tried to stop her, to comfort her. No one touched her. They waited.

Finally her mother took the cat, plush hair flattened, but still wearing a little smile, from Lana's hands and handed it back to the police officers.

"Lana, come into the living room. We need to talk to these men." Her mother pulled her away from the window, letting one of the men examine it.

"This window was not forced open," the tall, dark-skinned man said.

"I left it open for Seti to come in." Lana was ready to talk. "I couldn't find my cat when I came home. I left the window open so he could come in when he did return." She defended leaving herself vulnerable.

Seated in the living room, the officer, looking a bit foolish holding the stuffed cat, spoke again. "Do you have any idea who'd want to frighten you like this, Miss Richardson?"

"Someone put scorpions in her room the night before last," Mrs. Richardson told them. "We didn't call you then since it was obviously someone being malicious, but this was worse. Both acts have been deliberately planned to frighten Lana."

"I don't know how, or who, but I think all of this is somehow connected to the theft of the Egyptian necklace." Lana told the police as much of the story as she could come up with. What had happened was all so confusing to her. "Someone tried to frighten me at the museum the night before the exhibit opened. Then the necklace was stolen while I was there."

His partner took notes while Officer Dickenson asked the questions, what few he could think of. Mostly who might have done this, and Lana had no answer for that.

They stood up to leave. "I suggest you keep your window closed and locked, Miss Richardson."

"But what about Seti? He's still lost."

"If he comes home in this storm, he'll get under a bush or hide someplace until morning. Then he can come in the door. I have three cats. They have their hiding places." He smiled at Lana for the first time. "I can understand how this scared you. I can understand how the Egyptian people came to worship cats. I'm crazy about mine."

To have this large police officer confess that he loved cats himself made Lana start to cry again. This time quietly. She took the hand he offered and thanked him. Compared to drive-by shootings, muggings in the park, and some of the other calls he went on, this one was pretty tame. But he seemed to understand how she felt.

Sunday morning, at first light, Lana was awakened from a deep, dreamless sleep. It was the sleep of exhaustion, and she woke feeling heavy and disoriented. But something had awoken her.

She sat up, shook her head to clear it, then got up and flew to the window. Snow piled on the limbs of the huge cottonwood tree. The world was white.

Something tugged at her, forced her to grab her robe, slip her feet into her slippers, and run to the front door. A warm, magnetic force seemed to pull at her. She unlocked the door and jerked it open.

There on the front porch sat Seti. He didn't sit for long. The minute Lana pushed open the screen, he slipped through the narrowest of cracks and ran to the kitchen. Lana ran behind him.

"Seti," she cried. "Seti, where have you been? Are you all right? Let me see you."

Seti crunched a dry morsel of cat food and lapped water as if he was terribly thirsty. Then he looked up at Lana and smiled his tiny smile. She grabbed him into her arms and hugged him tight. He cooperated for a minute. Then he wiggled.

She set him back onto the floor, and he started eating again. Wherever he'd been, he hadn't eaten or had any water. But he wasn't wet like he would be had he stayed outside in the storm all night. Had someone trapped him and kept him prisoner while they played the awful trick on her?

She didn't know, but she sat beside Seti and rubbed his back while he ate.

Lana needed to stay inside and finish homework. She tried studying while Seti snuggled first on her lap, then moved to the bed for some serious sleeping.

By afternoon the sun was shining, melting

the fall snow quickly. For the first time, Lana wished she didn't have to go to the museum. But she was scheduled for the afternoon and evening shift. She couldn't let the staff down. One volunteer had the flu. Another was called out of town on an emergency. There weren't any substitutes available.

She hoped she didn't look as tired as she felt. And, at first, talking about the relics, telling the stories and myths about Egyptian culture, energized her.

The big news that Marge could hardly wait to tell her, the minute she arrived, was that the wedding necklace was back. Someone had returned the jewelry, actually placing it inside the glass case. The news hadn't been reported on TV or in the newspapers, but whispers spread among the huge crowds who were visiting the exhibit, and the necklace was what people wanted to see first.

"Why do you think it was returned?" a woman asked Lana as soon as she'd viewed it carefully. People huddled so close to Lana and the case, she felt smothered. She stepped behind the glass enclosure and leaned on it slightly.

"We don't know who took it, or why the thief decided to bring it back," she said. "We're just grateful to have it in the collection again.

We can send the exhibit back to Egypt intact, with not too many black marks against the museum."

She did have a strong opinion she didn't voice for the visitors. Having the necklace return the day after Antef Raam was shut into the coffin could not be coincidence. Surely he had taken it. Someone saw or knew he was guilty and used their own peculiar means to frighten him into returning it. As much as she deplored the theft, she was glad that Antef had this chance to undo his crime. This chance to keep from ruining his life and disgracing his family.

Antef was on duty at the exhibit today, smiling and more animated than ever. Was that relief she saw on his face? She couldn't make eye contact with him. She had to use her imagination.

The warm pull toward Nefra's coffin was the strongest it had ever been. Lana could have stood there all day. She moved quickly through her tour in order to spend extra time beside Nefra. She always positioned herself so she could stand right next to him, as well as see his likeness on his sarcophagus.

Love would be the word she'd use if someone asked her to describe her feelings. Her emotions were raw, resting right on the surface, so that might explain why she felt her love to be more powerful today. But love was an emotion she could handle.

"Your voice changes when you talk about Nefra and Urbena, Miss Richardson," a young woman said. "You are emotionally involved with their story, aren't you?"

No one had ever asked her such a question. No one had ever been so observant. She felt her face flame. She stared at Nefra instead of her audience and trusted her voice.

"You are very perceptive." She looked up then and smiled at the young woman.

"I'm a psychologist, trained to watch body language and listen to voices." She laughed. "I could even go so far as to say I think you are in love with this mummy, or maybe this king. But I would hate to embarrass you."

The crowd laughed. They knew Lana was already embarrassed. Her face grew hotter and suddenly she had to move away from Nefra. She led the group out of the exhibit. But she walked alongside the woman who had accused her of loving the young king.

"Do you think a person can tap into leftover emotion, even from thousands of years ago?" Lana asked softly.

"I'm open to most any idea about emotions, Miss Richardson, and to energy floating

around us, how it might bounce off these artifacts, carrying ancient feelings to those who
are open to feeling them."

"Would some people be more susceptible
to receiving those feelings than others?" Lana
dared ask.

"Of course. Lots of people walk through life
feeling as little as possible. Others seem to be
living magnets for the emotions around us."

The fact that the woman used the word Lana
had been using herself, magnetic, made Lana
listen even more carefully.

"But Lana," the woman used Lana's first
name, printed on her badge, "at the risk of
frightening you, if you can pick up positive
emotions, you can also pick up negative —
vibes — for lack of a better word. You said
earlier that Egyptian royal life was full of jealousy, murder, and the fight for power. Those
feelings may still surround these artifacts as
well. Take this ring, for instance." She
stopped at the last case before they reached
the entrance. The crowd had moved ahead of
them into the hall.

Lana was catching on. "If I wore it, I might
be able to feel what the original owner felt?"

"I believe it's possible. Some people would
say this is ridiculous, the result of my imagination, but I'm one of those people who can

read off metals. I can hold any piece of jewelry and receive emotions that the owner felt. Some are stronger than others. Depends on the events in the wearer's life. Negative emotions seem to hang onto metal longer and stronger."

"I wish I could let you hold the ring, but I don't have a key to the case, nor the authority for that. What you experienced would be fascinating, though," Lana said.

"You can see I like antique jewelry." The woman pointed to the pin and the ring she wore. "But I have to be very careful buying pieces. I held this ring for a long time before I bought it. And I have given back jewelry I knew I couldn't wear."

"Do you have a card?" Lana asked. "I'd like to talk to you more."

"Of course." The young woman fished in her huge denim bag and pulled out a slightly dog-eared business card. "Do call. I'd love to talk to you, to test you further. I think you're the most sensitive person I've come across in a long time."

Lana's collection of strange knowledge was growing by leaps and bounds. She stored the woman's words for further thought, and further reading, if she could locate reference material.

She muddled through guiding one more group, feeling nothing by now. Her own powers of receiving were dulled by exhaustion. Two nights with little sleep were taking effect. Marge had offered her a ride home and she accepted gratefully. She wished she was in the car now.

Taking a flashlight from one of the wall cupboards so she'd have extra light, she checked every case, shining the beam onto each shelf, checking, double-checking, as she prepared to close. She didn't even stop to say good night to Nefra the way she sometimes did. She hurried toward the first room. Just then the lights snapped off, plunging her into total darkness.

Her knees turned to water. She wanted to crumple to the floor. Not again, please no, not again.

Sure enough, the whispers echoed around her. But this time, near Nefra's coffin, a candle flared to life. The tiny flame was enough to allow her to see the figure standing beside the sarcophagus.

Raising both arms toward Lana, the mummy spoke. "Urbena, my princess. You must come back to me."

Come back, come back, come back. The words echoed around the corners of the hollow room.

"I do not wish to live again without you."

Chapter 18

One last surge of energy spurred Lana and sent her running for the door. It was closed. Locked. Turning her back on the apparition, she pounded frantically.

"Marge — Antef — someone, please! Please open the door!"

Pressing her back to the door, she pointed her flashlight and looked again in the direction of Nefra's coffin. On stiff, bandaged legs the mummy stumbled stiffly toward her. Hands reached for her. Eyes, dark sockets in the gauze-wrapped face stared. Where the mouth dented in slightly, a narrow slit let the mummy speak in a raspy whisper.

"Do not run away, Urbena. I need you. You can break the curse. Return to your coffin. Return to Egypt with me."

With the hand that held her light, she banged on the door, keeping both eyes glued on the shambling figure. Closer, closer, it moved, reaching for her. Her heart throbbed in her throat, choking her. She gripped the handle of her light. She could use the light for a weapon, but would it do any good to hit this — this thing.

This person. Her senses tried to return.

"Who are you? What do you want?" She forced out the voice from inside her, forced her words to come out without her voice shaking. "Why are you doing this to me?"

The mummy stopped walking toward her.

Lana pounded again on the door behind her. Her light flickered off, leaving her in blackness.

Suddenly the lock clicked and the door swung open. "Lana? How did you get locked in there?" Marge said. "Good thing I was looking for you. You could have ended up in there all night."

Antef held the key to the inside door. "I turned off the lights, Lana. Sorry. I thought everyone was out."

"I — I — " Lana looked into the dark room. Then she stepped back inside and tried the lights. Brightness flooded the room. She ran to Nefra's coffin. He lay still, hands crossed exactly right. He hadn't moved.

"Lana, what happened? You didn't just get

locked in there." Marge was the one who noticed that Lana had been frightened beyond the idea of spending a night in the museum.

Lana took a deep breath. "The mummy — the mummy — "

"You have seen the mummy move his hands again?" Antef asked.

"Nefra — someone dressed as Nefra was here, walking around, threatening me." Lana managed to get the words out.

Now Marge stared at Lana. "The mummy came after you?"

"I know it sounds crazy, Marge. It sounds crazy to me. But this is the second time it has happened. This — this thing," she pointed at Nefra, "followed me home one night."

Marge stared at Lana. Her face was white, her eyes solemn — for a few seconds. "Like a puppy?" A grin spread slowly across her face.

"I might have known no one would believe me. If you don't, Marge — if — oh, why did I bother telling you?"

"I'm sorry, Lana, I'm sorry. But if you could hear yourself." Marge looked worried. "I mean, those were the first words that popped into my mind. But this isn't funny. You are believing something impossible."

Despite her fear, Lana smiled. She heard her words over again herself. *A mummy followed me home.*

She remembered that she had read and loved so many picture books where dinosaurs, elephants, impossible animals followed kids home. And the first thing the kid said was, "Can I keep it?" To her dismay she started to cry.

"I'm taking you home, Lana." Marge took her arm. "Whatever happened to you, I can see you are still frightened. I'm going to see that you get inside your house in one piece. We can talk about this tomorrow in the daylight."

Dr. Walters and Blair Vaughn chose that moment to appear in the Egyptian exhibit. "Aren't you closing up, Antef? It's past hours. Lana, you still here? Marge?"

"We were just double-checking everything," Marge said quickly.

"Go ahead, then. I wanted to show Blair the necklace, and she wants to verify that it wasn't harmed."

"Someone could have substituted a copy for the real thing." Blair looked at Lana as if wondering what was going on. "Are you all right, Lana? You look awfully pale."

"Yes, sure. I'm tired. This has been a long weekend."

Lana hurried out of the interior room. She didn't want Antef or Marge to blurt out that Lana had seen a mummy walking toward her. She thought Blair had some respect for her, but it wouldn't take much to change that opinion.

"Don't forget the party next weekend," Dr. Walters called after them. "We have plenty to celebrate now that the collection is intact. And the volunteers have done a great job."

"How could we forget that this exhibit is closing at last?" Marge took Lana's arm and propelled her down the hall and out the side door where the guard waited to lock up behind them. "I've never worked so hard for no pay. This has been a tough show."

Lana couldn't think of anything to say. She could certainly agree. It had been a tough three weeks. And there was one week to go. A lot could happen in a week.

Despite her worries, nothing happened except that she got her official invitation to the closing party. Her mother got excited about the possibilities.

"It's a costume party." She clapped her hands. "Egyptian dress, of course. I'm going to make you a costume, Lana. And don't argue with me."

Lana's mother was so excited that Lana didn't try to argue. "That's great, Mom. Thank you. And Seti, make a costume for Seti. I've decided to take him with me. He gets along well with people. Make him a rhinestone collar, and I'll put a leash on it. I'll be a queen and he can be my good-luck charm."

Lana had clung to Seti all week, needing extra warmth and loving. There was something about Seti curling next to her on the bed at night, greeting her at the door every day, just being there for Lana, that made her feel special.

And safe. Don't forget safe.

I'm not going to feel safe until next week, a small voice inside her replied. But just as she started to relax and look forward to the party, she had another dream and received another note.

Chapter 19

I walk beside him. Crowds line both sides of the road, holding branches of olive and palm, waving them slowly, and cheering, always cheering.

The train of my wedding dress is carried by two attendants. My crown is heavy, but I hold my head high. After a short distance my neck begins to ache, but if this is the price of happiness, I can bear it willingly. With joy.

He turns and smiles at me. His dark eyes dance and tease and remind me of his gentleness. Real strength comes from being kind and just and most of all gentle, aware of others. He is already popular. He will be a fine king.

He has not come to this by stealth or revenge or evil events. He has inherited the throne from his father, who was also well loved.

I wave at the crowds. I will work hard to win their respect and love, just as I won Nefra's admiration. From the first time he saw me, he says.

I stop to receive a bouquet of flowers from a child in a long white dress. The child smiles, bowing her ebony hair, tilting the circlet of wild flowers so it slides over her forehead. With her small hand she catches it, grins, more childlike now.

I turn to find that Nefra has continued walking without me. Where is he? Crowds have closed in behind him so I cannot see.

"Nefra," I call in a soft voice. "Nefra." The crowds realize what they have done. They step aside, leaving a path. But still I do not see him.

"Nefra," I call louder. "Nefra!"

He is gone, disappeared from my sight. I reach out, run, glance both ways with a growing fear.

"Nefra!" I scream his name now. My words echo back across the heads of the people.

The crowd does not help me find Nefra, but people close about me, tighter, tighter, smothering me. Keeping me from him.

"He is gone," someone whispers. "Nefra is gone."

Gone. Gone. Gone. Gone.

Lana sat up, feeling a terrible loss. Her arms were empty, cold. The deep, secure warmth she had felt was replaced by icy daggers stabbing her all over.

"Gone," she whispered and started to cry.

Seti woke and stood looking at her, his eyes golden and puzzled. She gathered him in her arms and hugged him so tight he protested and wiggled loose. Jumping to the floor, he looked back and meowed.

She hadn't wakened until morning, but the light coming from her window was strange, gray, and foreboding. How can light be foreboding, she scolded herself. The dream is coloring the light. Today was the last day of the exhibit. The museum would close early for the party. She and her mother had worked late to finish her dress and Seti's rhinestone collar. Tonight was going to be special.

Nothing felt special. The feeling she had brought to the beginning of the exhibit was gone. Replaced by fear and puzzlement and — and loss. A longing for something that no longer existed. If it ever did. She felt hollow inside, bereft.

"It's still snowing," her mother said, as Lana and Seti entered the kitchen. Seti pranced and meowed until Lana opened a can of cat food for him. He hunched before his dish and nibbled daintily, looking up often to squint his eyes.

"He could make those cat-food commercials where the long-haired sophisticated Persian eats from a crystal goblet." Mrs. Richardson laughed. "Wonder how much they pay? I could quit my job and become his trainer."

"Mother," Lana scolded. "Surely you wouldn't take advantage of a helpless animal."

"Seti is about as helpless as a Siberian tiger."

Seti left a few bites of food in his bowl and started to wash his paws and face.

Lana couldn't eat all her breakfast, either. After a few bites, she gave up and hurried to dress. She was glad she was working this morning. She could come back home, take her time getting ready for the party, and get Seti.

Josh had agreed to take her. While he wasn't sold on antiquities, he did like parties, even parties with mostly adults present. Lana also suspected he was glad to celebrate the end of the exhibit so he'd see more of her.

"Wow, you look terrific, Lana." Josh stepped back when Lana opened the door that evening. His expression of admiration backed up his words. "I've heard everyone say you look Egyptian, but I couldn't see it until tonight."

"It's the dress." Lana had stared at her own

image in the mirror for a long time. Her dress was similar to the white, pleated one she had been wearing in her dream, except that the neck was plain instead of having a gold collar. The fabric was a sheer white cotton that looked handwoven.

Her mother was a genius with a sewing machine and had great taste in fabrics. She didn't get to be head buyer for Foley's women's departments for no reason. Not only had she designed and sewn the dress, but she had made a small drawstring bag that tied around the waist to match, since Lana wouldn't have handmaidens to carry her comb and lipstick, a handkerchief, and her door key.

Lana had studied pictures, then made up her face with the extended black eyeliner, like kohl, that made eyes look huge. Green shadow on her lids was exaggerated, and she wore more lipstick than usual. She hardly recognized herself.

"You're going to take this cat?" Josh looked at Seti with little enthusiasm, but having Lana on his arm made up for Seti.

"Oh, yes, and I forgot to cut his nails." She grabbed Seti and held him tightly in her lap. He wiggled and squirmed like mad. "Help me, Josh. He didn't complain a minute when I put that collar and leash on him. I want to cut his nails so he won't tear anyone's dress or stockings."

Josh knelt down to help Lana hold Seti. That made him protest even more. "It's okay, Seti," Josh said. "No cat likes his nails trimmed. You're normal after all."

Lana grabbed one waving paw and squeezed Seti's claws out one by one. "Most cats would have had a fit about wearing a collar, unless they were trained to it from a kitten. 'Course I told him what we were going to do and explained why all the fuss was necessary."

Josh shook his head. "Sure you did. And he said, 'Just this once, for you.' You and I have one thing in common, old boy." Josh patted Seti on the head when his nails were almost finished. "We'll both make fools of ourselves occasionally because we like this woman."

"There, Seti. Good grief." Lana turned Seti loose and shoved the fingernail clippers into the small purse at her waist. Seti glared first at Lana, then at Josh.

"Don't laugh at him," Lana warned. "Cats don't like to be laughed at."

"Neither do I, Seti, but look at me."

Josh had wrapped a few boxfuls of gauze around his jeans and T-shirt until he achieved a very loose interpretation of being a mummy. He'd done a better job of wrapping the top of his head, but left two strips of gauze hanging down in the back like a tail.

"If we have to, Seti, we'll unwind some of that bandage on his arms and put it around his mouth." Lana tried to tease Josh, tried to be excited, to lift the heavy mood she had carried all day. She tugged at Seti's leash, letting him walk to the door. Then he was glad to be carried because of the snow.

"Drive carefully, Josh," Mrs. Richardson said, after looking Lana over one more time.

"I will. The back streets aren't cleared, but the main arteries have been plowed. And it's not far. We could have walked."

"A princess doesn't wade through snow-drifts." Lana had pulled on her boots and carried her sandals in a plastic bag. "I don't think it snows much in Egypt, either."

Seti rode in her lap and now seemed excited. Instead of curling up and taking a quick nap, he sat straight and stared at the windshield wipers. Occasionally he glanced out the side window, as if he was looking for something in particular.

Josh let them off at the door, then drove around to park the car. "Meet you inside."

"Fine. I want to change shoes and leave my coat in my locker. That way I can make a more regal grand entrance."

Josh laughed and drove away through the slush in the museum lot.

Lana hurried to the back of the museum. She still carried Seti. She'd walk him on his leash later.

Slipping off her coat, she pulled the leash strap over her wrist that wasn't laden with jingling bracelets. She replaced the boots with sandals. Only then did she spin her combination lock and open the small locker in the employees' lounge.

"What's this, Seti?" She bent to pick up the paper that fluttered to the floor.

Her heart raced. The same printing, same block letters. And a similar message. The same nightmare. Would it ever end? She had a terrible foreboding about the evening to come as she read the words.

URBENA, MY PRINCESS. YOU MUST COME
   BACK TO ME.
I DO NOT WISH TO LIVE AGAIN WITHOUT
   YOU.
TONIGHT. THE TIME IS TONIGHT.
IT IS OUR LAST CHANCE. PLEASE COME
   TO ME.

NEFRA

Chapter 20

"Are you all right?" Josh was waiting for her as he promised, but he was too perceptive. Should she tell him about the note, show it to him? She hadn't told him anything else so far. Why hadn't she shared her fears, all the things that had been happening to her, with Josh? She wasn't sure. Maybe because he hadn't been a part of this whole Egyptian experience from the beginning. Surely he would care, but . . . something held her back.

"Sure, fine. Just stay close to me this evening, will you, Josh? Promise." She took his arm, letting Seti down to walk, wrapping his leash over her wrist.

"Don't worry about that. I'd planned to. You look too great. I have to protect my interests."

Lana felt she was having to pay too great a price for *her* interests. Was Darrah right? The Egyptian culture carried with it an overload of mystery and magic. There was certainly something awesome and occasionally frightening about being around the relics.

But aside from the disturbing dreams, her fascination with Nefra and his mummy, Lana knew there was a human factor involved here. A real, live person was trying to frighten her. A human hand had written the notes she and Antef had gotten. A human hand had placed scorpions in her room, wrapped the pseudo-cat mummy and tried to frighten her with it. And surely there was a human being inside the mummy who had walked in the park. Despite all the old movies she had seen, she could not believe that Nefra had risen from his coffin to walk about and frighten her.

As she walked into the party, she knew she was going to look at each person and think, *Is it you, is it you, is it you?*

The minute they reached the third-floor rooms where the party was in progress, people turned to stare at her. Some smiled, others murmured surprise. Many eyes held admiration. Lana wasn't used to being admired, but she found she liked it. The feeling helped balance the shaking in her stomach, the wobble in her knees. She put on a happy face and pretended to be at ease. Josh knew. He knew.

He placed his hand over hers, resting on his arm, and squeezed.

"Lana, you look incredible." Blair Vaughn was the first to actually approach her. "I told you the first time I met you that you looked like Urbena. Tonight you *are* Urbena." Blair laughed and looked down at Seti. "And that cat. Where did you find it? It has true royal blood, I'm sure." She bent to stroke Seti, but the cat stepped away from her, twisting around Lana's ankles, so that she had to bend to untangle him.

When Lana stood up, Blair was gone, but across the room Lana saw Blair point a man in Lana's direction.

"Miss, do you mind if we take a photo?" the man said, coming up to Lana. "I'm from the *Rocky Mountain News*, covering the party."

"Well, I think — I'd rather you wouldn't right now."

David Walters rescued her. "Lana, you look perfect. I have a splendid idea." He turned to the reporter-photographer. "Follow us. I'll get you a photo you won't forget."

Lana resisted going with Dr. Walters for a few seconds. She looked at Josh, who shrugged. "Will you hold Seti?"

Josh took the leash and followed Lana from

a distance. Dr. Walters steered Lana into the second exhibit room. "I owe you an apology, Lana. I never really thought you took the necklace when it was stolen, but I was terribly upset. You can understand that. I'm responsible for all of these artifacts. Anyway, to make up for it, I want you to wear it tonight. That costume demands a lovely piece of jewelry."

"Oh, I couldn't." Lana had a terrible fear of even touching the necklace, much less wearing it. It would be heavy, if would hold those feelings the psychologist had talked to her about.

David Walters was persistent, plus he had seen a chance for good publicity. "It will be safe. No one is going to stop looking at you all evening anyway. You could have stepped out of the nineteenth dynasty." Dr. Walters opened the case and had the necklace out before Lana could protest more. He placed it around her neck.

She cradled the weight in both hands while he lifted her hair and fastened the clasp.

"Stunning, just stunning." Walters clapped his hands together in delight.

Flashbulbs popped from several directions. No one was any longer asking her permission. No one could resist taking pictures of her wearing the wedding gift from Nefra.

In seconds, however, Lana was hardly

aware of the attention she was getting. A warmth like nothing she'd ever felt, deeper, more stirring than that she'd received near Nefra's coffin, surrounded her, seeped into her skin, filled her inside, putting her in a trance-like stupor.

Finally, fighting to regain her own persona, to become Lana again, she looked up to find Antef staring at her. "Bad luck, Lana." He shook his head. "Everyone who touches that piece is cursed or is dead."

Josh had followed Lana and said angrily, "Of course they're dead. No one has worn it for thousands of years. Ignore him, Lana. The necklace completes your costume. It could have been made for you."

"All that curse business is superstition." Marge showed up to comment on Lana's appearance. "Those emerald stones match your eyes, Lana. You look incredibly beautiful tonight." Although Marge wore a gown similar to Lana's, she had a plump, matronly look. "I think I'll have to play the role of queen-mother."

Lana grabbed Marge's hand. "Come with me, Marge. I have to see the necklace for myself."

Two more flashbulbs went off on their way down the hall to the bathroom. "I wish they'd stop that," Lana said. "They're making me even more nervous."

"You asked for it, Lana, looking like you do. But hey, it's fun. And surely people will send you copies of the photos. You'll have them to remind you of the exhibit."

Lana was certain she'd need no reminders of the last four weeks. The exhibit. This party.

She stopped, awed by her own image in the bathroom mirror. The necklace did complete her costume.

"If I didn't believe in reincarnation before, I could now." Marge laughed.

Lana continued to stare, grasped the cold basin, tried to breathe normally.

Come to me. Tonight. Tonight is our last chance. Come with me and be my queen.

She shivered. Suddenly the necklace felt heavy, like thick rope and heavy boulders around her neck. The metal burned her flesh and the mesh cut into her skin. She lifted it and longed to take it off, leave it here on the counter, come back for it later.

"Marge, I have to find Josh. See you outside." Lana whirled around and left the rest room, practically running down the hall toward the murmur of voices, the tinkle of glasses, laughter, lots and lots of people.

"Where's Seti?" She noticed he was off the

leash the minute she found Josh.

"I don't know. I didn't even know he was gone for a few minutes. I'm sorry, Lana. Someone must have released the clip on his collar when I wasn't looking."

"We have to find him." Her heart leaped and pounded in her throat. She fought the panic that churned her stomach.

"He'll be all right. He was letting everyone hold him. He likes people. Someone is probably holding him right now. I'll help you look."

They found him almost immediately. Darrah held him in her arms. He wasn't struggling, but he looked aloof, uninterested in being petted.

"Oh, Darrah, thank goodness you found him." Lana reached for the leash.

"He found me, actually. He rubbed on my ankles until I picked him up. I think he wanted to be where he could see." Darrah smiled at Lana, acting as if she'd forgotten she'd ever threatened Lana. Maybe she felt secure because she was with Rod tonight.

"I think he was looking for you, Lana." Rod wore a classic costume of ancient Egypt, complete with a rounded gold headpiece with a cobra rising from the front. He should have looked foolish in the short skirt, but he didn't. His legs were tan and muscled, cuffed at the ankle with what looked like pure gold.

Dr. Walters searched for Lana again. "Lana, come in here. You, too, Rod. Pose together. With that cat. Is that your cat, Lana? Perfect touch."

Walters had pulled them toward a group of reporters before Lana could protest. "Publicity, Lana. Think publicity," Walters whispered.

She tried. For Dr. Walters' sake. For the museum, which always needed donations. In a few minutes, though, she started to wish she had never worn a costume. Had never tried to look like an Egyptian princess. The novelty had worn off. The fun was gone.

As soon as she could manage, she slipped away. Refreshments were in the hall, and people tended to gather around the wine and cheese, the coffee and sweets. She was relieved to find a few minutes of peace in the back room of the exhibit. She needed to visit with Nefra. She *had* to.

Come to me, my queen. Come. Come.

She needed to look at Nefra's mummy, his image on his coffin, one more time. She needed to let him see the necklace. As soon as the idea entered her head, it frightened her. She realized how much she had come to think of him as a person, alive today, making his presence felt.

He loves me.

She stopped, startled by that thought. Nefra loved Urbena. I am *not* Urbena.

You belong to me. I need you with me. Come. Come.

She shook her head to clear the voice that spoke to her unbidden. But slowly her feet moved toward his coffin. The force that surrounded it pulled at her like a whirlpool that would suck her in, spin her around, carry her away.

She stopped six feet away. Four. Then took the final step. She clutched the edge of the coffin and looked inside.

For seconds her mind refused to register what she saw. Not possible — not possible — not possible. Common sense ruled.

She held her breath until her chest ached. Dizzy, she leaned over, placed her hand flat on the smooth wood inside the casket. The box was empty.

I knew you would come. The voice whispered beside her, just out of her peripheral vision. *Tonight you must come with me. This is our last chance for happiness.*

She didn't want to turn around, but he insisted, his mind gently demanding. She turned, stared.

His partially unwrapped face was godlike in its beauty. His dark eyes held admiration and the same deep love *she* had felt over and over, here and in her dreams.

Holding out both arms, his long fingers bare, strong, he reached for her. *You must not be afraid. We belong together.*

And then he touched her.

Her legs crumpled. In slow motion she sank to the cool, marble floor. One last thought registered before she passed out.

His touch was warm, oh so humanly warm.

Chapter 21

When Lana regained consciousness, she didn't know where she was. She was no longer crumpled in a heap on the museum floor. When she tried to move, she couldn't.

She squirmed, thrashed, wiggled. She threw her body back and forth, but all she could do was rock. Breathe, she told herself, breathe. In and out, in and out, she filled her lungs, exhaled, kept a rhythm until she felt calm.

The lights were out in the back room. Maybe someone would come in, would notice that it was dark. But what if they didn't? She couldn't call out. Something was across her mouth.

She was tied up. *No, wrapped up.* She could move her fingers enough to feel the texture of the material that kept her rigid. Gauze, bandage gauze.

At the same time that she made that discovery, her eyes adjusted a little to the darkness.

No, please, no.

She was lying inside something. Smooth walls. Wrapped in gauze like a mummy. Someone had made her into a living mummy.

Urbena's coffin. She was inside the coffin made for the princess. That was the only empty coffin in the show.

Nefra — no, that was impossible.

Come back with me. Tonight is your last chance.

I won't! she screamed silently and struggled against the gauze. She could shift her hands and arms, crossed over her chest and ribs, but the bandages held her just as tightly as any rope or chain.

For a few more seconds she lay still, forcing herself to breathe, trying to think about what to do. The thought that came to her, though, had nothing to do with how to get loose. She wanted to know who had done this to her, who had wrapped her up and placed her in this coffin.

Nefra? — No, Nefra did not do this to her. She shuddered as she remembered his touch. Could — could her imagination have run so wild that she thought she saw him, felt his touch? Who — ?

The mummy — the man under the bandages — looked like she had imagined Nefra; he looked just like the image on his coffin, even though that picture was stylized in the Egyptian manner.

Forget Nefra for now. I must escape. She forced her mind to return to her immediate problem. Not whether the man she had seen was six thousand years old. Not even whether he had placed her here or someone else had done it for him. But how to get loose.

She needed something sharp. Her purse! What was in her purse? Sliding her hand up and down slightly, she loosened the gauze enough to allow her wrist to lie flat against her waist. Then she wiggled until she could feel the roll of the drawstring with the little finger of her left hand.

Concentrate. Her hand was tighter against her waist in this position, but she had to slip her fingers over, under the drawstring. The first time she did it, the string slid away from her.

Patience. Just hook your finger around and press the string against your waist to get a grip on it.

She was grateful for the roughness of the cotton. The texture gave her a better grip on the drawstring.

Little by little she bunched up the string and pushed it under her hand. Her thumb could wiggle enough to pull the cloth up and up and up until her finger touched the top of the bag.

All of the fingers in her left hand began to cramp. She flexed them as much as possible and forced them to relax. Then she tugged at the small, cloth bag again.

When she had the top bunched under her hand, she rubbed her little finger over the rest of the pouch.

The clippers! The fingernail clippers she had used to cut Seti's nails. Without thinking, she had dropped them into her bag. If she could wiggle them out, she could use them to cut the gauze. The cloth was thin, and she should be able to slice through it easily.

This was taking forever. Why hadn't anyone come looking for her? In the distance she could hear the tinkle of glasses, a low gathering of laughter. People having fun, enjoying the party. No one realized she was gone.

While she rested her hand, she sent mental messages to Josh and Seti. *Seti, come. Come find me, Seti.* She figured she could reach Seti before she could Josh. She and Seti were the ones with the mind connection. *Come, Seti, come.*

And what good will it do if Seti comes here and finds me? He will probably leap up and sit on my chest. Meow and say what are you doing in there. Get out and pet me.

She almost started to giggle, then realized she was losing control. Her laughter was coming from hysteria. Get back to work, Lana. Help yourself. You need to hurry. Where was the person who put her here? What purpose did placing her in the coffin serve? Surely this was not some sick joke, someone's idea of a prank.

Her hand stopped cramping. She wiggled her fingers again and slid her little finger down to examine the pouch, locate the clippers. Once her finger hooked around them, she pressed as hard as she could and slid. Pressed and slid, pressed and slid. Slowly she worked the clippers up to the mouth of the purse.

Now she must be careful. If she slid the clippers out and they slipped away from her, she could never reach them. Up and up and up until finally she held them in her hand against her ribs. She poked the point of the clippers under a strip of gauze and pushed as hard as she could. Finally it tore through. Tearing that one strip didn't seem to help at all. The process was slow, too slow. But it was working. Snipping the bandage, clipping more and more, she was finally starting to feel she could escape. With her hands free, she could peel the gauze off her mouth and yell for help, or she could keep peeling and get out of the coffin by herself.

Just as she started cutting the last strip that held her right hand, she heard footsteps. She froze, holding her breath. Was someone looking for her? If so, why didn't they turn on the lights? Call out?

As the footsteps approached the coffin, she wiggled and moaned, groaned, yelped, made as much noise as possible with her mouth covered over.

The low laughter stopped her. This was not someone looking for her. This was someone coming back to finish what they had started.

First, hands unclasped the necklace from around her neck, removed it. Hands rough against her throat, a man's hands. A man's smell. Antef! It was Antef!

She tried to call his name, to protest. "Uuuuummmmm."

The voice she had heard before whispered, "Mine, you are all mine, Urbena. Now you can return to Egypt with me. The curse will be broken."

As frightened as she was, she faced an even greater terror. The coffin lid made a scraping noise as he lifted it and rested it sideways on the coffin.

Then with a rasp and a screech that set her heart thudding down to her toes, the lid slid into place, closing her inside.

Chapter 22

The darkness was absolute. A stale, musty odor surrounded her, coming from the old wood. For a few seconds panic again sucked away all the air in the coffin. She choked, feeling as if the lid rested on her chest, squeezing, squeezing.

She remembered the scorpions and thought she heard them scraping along the edges of the wood, brushing against her body. She thought she felt their cold, hard pods against her cheek and she dared not move.

She remembered the dream, the sound of clods of dirt hitting the top of the coffin as someone began to fill the grave. *I'm not dead!* she screamed. *I'm not dead. Don't bury me, please don't bury me.*

Squeezing her eyes shut, she fought the images, fought the impulse to scream, even though her mouth was bound.

She hadn't the slightest chance of escaping if she lost control. Breathe, breathe deeply.

No air. No air, choking, hot. She coughed, squeezed her eyes tighter, and let herself yell and scream, if only in her imagination. What came out was "um-um-um."

Then she forced a regular rhythm of breathing. Put herself into a meditative state until she could think.

She found the clippers still in her hand. Finished tearing and ripping off the gauze from her hands. As soon as her hands were free, she tore the cloth from her mouth.

And screamed for real. No one would hear her, but there was some satisfaction in the act, the sound reverberating around her in the closed space. Screaming used up the air, sucked it away, leaving little for survival.

She calmed herself again and pushed against the lid. With all her strength she placed both hands flat against the rough inner lid and pushed upward.

The heavy lid didn't rise at all, didn't shift out of place. It was firmly set on the coffin.

She forced down the panic, forced herself to lie still and think. Concentrate. The words that came surprised her.

Nefra, please, please let me go. I cannot return with you. I am not of your time. I am not your queen. I feel your love, but I cannot return it. I cannot help you. You do not want me to die. I know this. I feel your warmth, your strength, and I beg you to use your powers to help me. Help me, Nefra, please help me.

She breathed again, sensing less air, but knowing she must use what was available slowly, without panic.

"Josh, help me," she whispered, knowing they did not have the mind connection that she had with Nefra, with Seti.

Seti. She knew without question that her hope lay with Seti. She concentrated on the sleek black cat, placing a strong image of him in her mind.

Seti, please hear me. You must help me. You can help me. You are my only hope now. I need you. You have needed me, and now I need you. Come to me, Seti, please come.

Come. Come. Come. She let the single word repeat over and over in her mind. Then, *Seti, come. Seti, come.*

At last she heard his nails on the roof of her prison, scratching, digging on the lid.

She scratched back. "Seti, Seti, is it you?"

Hope rose in her, filling her mind, her body, with relief.

She heard the scrape of the coffin lid as it

slid sideways. Fresh air poured in and tears escaped down her cheeks.

She sat up, rolled over and out of the coffin forgetting her legs were still bound up in the gauze. She fell into Josh's arms. She hugged him, never wanting to let go.

Until she remembered. "Seti." She stooped and picked up the small cat, holding him tightly in her arms. "Oh, Seti, you heard me. You came."

"It was crazy, Lana," Josh said, still not asking how she came to be prisoner in the coffin. "Suddenly Seti went crazy. He meowed and tugged and pulled at the leash until I bent and snapped it off his collar. Setting him free seemed the right thing to do. Thank God, I followed my intuition."

"He came to me."

"He ran. I had to run to keep up. He ran into the dark room. I stopped to find the lights. By then he was on top of this — this coffin, digging into the lid like mad."

"I had been looking for you," Marge stood beside them. Lana hadn't even known she was there. "I saw Josh and Seti take off and followed."

"I couldn't have lifted off that lid by myself." Josh put his hand on Marge's shoulder.

"Want to tell us what you're doing playing mummy, Lana?" Marge helped Lana tear off the rest of the gauze strips that circled her body.

"I don't know. Someone — someone — " She decided not to tell them that she thought Nefra was standing beside her. That he touched her. They would think she had become crazed inside the coffin, that her imagination had run away again. "I guess I fainted. I remember crumpling onto the floor. When I came to, I was in — inside here. Then someone else came along and put the lid on top of me."

This did not explain much to Josh and Marge and their faces reflected their concern, but also their disbelief. Their questions that Lana could not answer.

But she knew one thing. She bent and placed Seti on the floor, started for the other room where the party still bubbled with people unaware of the drama going on in the next room.

"The necklace, Lana." Marge noticed that Lana was not wearing the priceless jewelry. "Where — "

"That's what I plan to find out." Lana strode toward the next room, searching for Antef.

He saw her coming and tried to hold his place, talking to three women dressed as Cleopatra. But his face showed anxiety, then fear. He turned and ran.

Lana was ready for that. She dashed after him and grabbed his arm. "You. I know it was you, Antef. I smelled that distinctive scent you've chosen to wear. You took the necklace from me. You put me in that coffin."

"No, no, Lana." Antef struggled but Lana found strength in anger. She held him firmly.

Dr. Walters walked up behind her. "Lana, what's wrong?"

"Antef took the necklace, Dr. Walters. For the second time. I'm sure of it. He can't have taken it far. He took it from me tonight. He's hidden it here someplace."

"Are you sure, Lana? Antef — "

"I'm sure." Lana stared at Antef. His face — his fear — told her all she needed to know.

Antef collapsed in a heap, sobbing. "I took the jewels. But I put them back. The necklace is cursed. I was cursed. I put it back."

"But then you took it again, Antef." Lana coaxed the story from the man. "What made the curse go away? What persuaded you that it was safe to steal the necklace a second time?"

"She promised. She said if I help her — She could not lift the coffin lid by herself — She promised — "

Lana swung around to see who Antef was accusing. A huge circle of guests, like a tribunal of Egyptian citizens ready to make accusations against an evil king at his funeral, gathered behind her and Antef.

She realized that Seti sat beside her, his eyes searching the crowd as well. She knelt beside him.

"Help me, Seti. Who is it?"

The sleek black cat stood and darted into the crowd. Blair Vaughn faded back against a group of people, but Seti singled her out. Running backward, she stumbled and fell, threw out both hands to protect herself.

"No, no, leave me alone."

Seti arched his back, hissed and spit as he crept closer to the frightened woman. Like a tiger stalking his prey, Seti closed in. Ears flattened, tail twitching, he prepared to attack.

"Don't let him near me!" Blair screamed. "No, Nefra, no, leave me alone!"

Chapter 23

Lana knelt and stroked Seti's fur flat, calming the cat. "It's all right, Seti. We have her. Don't hurt her."

But Lana felt terribly puzzled. Blair Vaughn had been the one? Why? Blair was the last person Lana would have suspected.

"Lana, is Antef saying that Blair is involved with the theft of the necklace?" Dr. Walters walked up behind Lana. Blair was crumpled into a heap on the floor, whimpering.

"Dr. Walters," Lana said, determined to sort this out, "there has been more going on than the theft. Someone has been terrorizing me, and tonight someone tied me up and put me in Urbena's coffin. I think this has something to do with the story that returning Urbena to her coffin will break the curse on her tomb."

"It will! You *will* break the curse!" Blair

screamed at Lana. "You are Urbena, you know you are. And if I could have returned you to Egypt and the tomb, my family would stop dying. I had you in her coffin, even though I had to bribe that stupid Antef into helping me. Why didn't you stay there?" Blair's eyes blazed with anger and frustration at not accomplishing what she had set out to do. Lana shivered at the rage directed at her. And the idea that Blair really did plan to put Lana, in Urbena's coffin, back into Urbena's tomb.

"What do you mean, Blair?" Lana questioned. "You *know* the curse isn't real. You know it's superstition. You told me that yourself."

"It *is* real. I told you that to keep you from discovering my plan. I know the curse is real. My grandfather died after he found Urbena's tomb. Then my father disappeared, and now my sister is missing in Cairo. The curse will go on and on unless I can return Urbena's mummy. You were perfect."

Dr. Walters' voice was always quiet, but now his tone was soothing, not unlike the way he'd talk to an unreasonable child.

"Blair, your grandfather wandered out into the desert alone. He was ill with a high fever, delirious. Granted, his body was never found, but you know he was sick."

"I don't know that. I'm looking for him. The sale of Urbena's necklace would have brought me the money I needed to return to Egypt and look for him. My sister, too. I must look for my sister." Blair got to her knees as if ready to run. Her eyes were glazed with the obsession she had for finding her sister and her grandfather's body.

"I checked on your sister after you told me she had left home, Blair. Your mother is certain that she ran away to get married. She may have contacted your mother by now. We can call Cairo, tonight if you like."

"No! I must go there. I must go back to Egypt now!" Blair screamed at them, curled herself into a ball, and then got deadly quiet.

"What about her father?" Lana whispered.

"He died of a heart attack. Years ago. Mrs. Vaughn remarried. But apparently Blair has never believed her father died. She was in this country going to college when it happened. She wasn't able to return for the funeral, so I guess it isn't real for her."

"I'm so sorry." Instead of being angry with Blair, Lana found she felt sorry for the woman. "What will happen now?"

"I'll have to get her into some kind of hospital. She'll be under the care of a psychiatrist. Perhaps she can recover from this breakdown.

The woman has a brilliant mind."

Lana didn't realize that Antef was standing beside her until he spoke. A guard stood beside him, holding his arm. "I cannot leave without saying that I'm sorry, Lana. I'm so very sorry."

"You were the one who pushed me and stole the necklace."

"Yes, I was very foolish. My family will be so ashamed."

"Then Blair frightened you into returning it?"

"Yes, she put me in that coffin to scare me. But then she changed her mind. She said if I would help her return you to Egypt in Urbena's coffin, I could take the necklace back from you. I could have half the money. She said *I* would be cursed if I didn't help her."

"Return Urbena's coffin with me inside," Lana said, shuddering again at the memory.

"I am so sorry." Antef hung his head.

"You are so stupid." Blair had been listening. She screamed at him.

"You are the one who stupidly angered Nefra by pretending to be his mummy, Blair Vaughn." Antef wasn't going to take all the blame for Blair's actions. But what did he mean by making Nefra angry?

"Lana was so easy to frighten, thinking

Nefra had come alive. Running from his mummy." Blair laughed, but it wasn't normal laughter. It was the same laughter from the foggy night in the park.

"You put those scorpions in my room, too, didn't you?" Lana's sympathy was gone. "You left the notes. You took Seti and left the cat mummy to frighten me."

"Yes, yes, yes. That stupid cat."

To Lana's surprise Seti, at her feet, hissed and strained at his leash. Blair leaned back, her arm covering her face. She was afraid of Seti.

"Where did she get scorpions?" Darrah's voice behind her surprised Lana.

Rod, standing beside Darrah, answered Darrah's question. "You can get scorpions at most big pet stores."

Lana felt she had to apologize to Rod. "Rod, Blair tried to make me believe you and Darrah were behind the threats I was getting. I'm sorry I believed her, even for a short time."

"You don't owe me any apology, Lana. You were frightened. And I — " Rod lowered his voice. "Darrah needs a friend right now. I — "

"I understand, Rod." Lana still liked Rod, but she had a lot of thinking to do about all that had happened. "We'll talk later. I'd like to be friends with Darrah, too. Josh and I will get together with both of you soon."

Rod understood what Lana was saying. He smiled and hugged her, then took Darrah's arm and pulled her away toward where other party goers stood, watching, wondering what was happening.

Lana had one more question for Blair. "Why did you dress up in that mummy suit and try to frighten me earlier this evening, Blair? Because I got away last time?"

"I didn't. I had almost given up. Then I found you lying there unconscious, and I knew I'd been given one last chance."

If that wasn't Blair, Lana thought, then who? Who else had pretended to be Nefra tonight? Or — or — The other possibility was too impossible to believe. Wasn't it?

And the night she had woken up to see him? Thinking she was still dreaming. Knowing she wasn't.

"Lana, are you all right?" Marge took her arm.

"Yes. Yes. Sure." Never, Lana added to herself.

The museum had extra security for the exhibit and the party. Dr. Walters motioned for two guards to take charge of Blair until she could be hospitalized and some proper place could be found for her long-term care.

When the uniformed man and woman took her arms, Blair fought them like Seti would fight if cornered. She screamed and tossed her long hair wildly about her face.

"You were perfect," Blair screamed at Lana again as the guards dragged her away. "You would have satisfied the gods. Nefra would have been pleased."

Lana stepped back and shivered again. She knew Blair was right. She knew Nefra would be pleased with her. He had told her so himself. She felt Josh's arm cradle her shoulders. Seti rubbed at her ankles.

"Can you forgive her, Lana?" Marge asked.

"Of course, Marge. She's not herself. All the suffering, all the losses she has experienced, have twisted her mind."

"But Antef was just greedy." Marge pointed to where two more guards led Antef away to wait for the police.

"He's so young," Lana said, trying to understand. "Maybe he was given too much responsibility too soon."

Marge took Lana's arm, linking her own through it. "I'm going to walk with Lana to get her coat and boots, Josh. I suspect she's had enough excitement for tonight."

"That's for sure." Lana was perfectly willing

to leave the party. She stooped and picked up Seti, cradled him in her arms. "Seti found me. I knew you could, Seti. Thank you. Thank you."

She kissed Seti on the top of his head, hearing the faint purr.

"Did you hear what Blair said when Seti attacked her, Lana? She called him Nefra. What do you think she meant by that?"

"I think she didn't know what she was saying," Lana answered. "She knew she was caught, that her plan to return Urbena, well, me instead of Urbena, was foiled."

Josh took Lana home, kissed her with extra warmth, and said he hoped life would return to normal. The museum staff packed up the exhibit in order to return it to Cairo with all the artifacts intact. But on the next Monday, the day before the relics were shipped, Lana had to rethink Blair's words.

That night, Seti, still wearing the beautiful rhinestone collar from the party, demanded to be let out through the window. Lana gave in. The weather had cleared and more Indian summer days were in progress. The night was warm and clear.

Seti paused in the window and looked at Lana for a long time. Lana returned his stare.

He wore that look she was sure was a tiny smile. She saw and felt the love in his eyes. And she returned that love. In fact, she grabbed him, squeezed him, and kissed the top of his head again before she let him go.

"Be careful, Seti. I love you." She watched him leap to the limb of the big tree closest to her window. He turned again and meowed. Then he scampered down, out of sight.

She felt terribly sad when he didn't return in the night. Nor did he come when she called from the back door next morning.

"He's on an exploring trip," her mother assured her. "He'll be here when you come home from school."

Somehow Lana didn't think so. Seti had come to her with the exhibit. He had left when the exhibit left. What did that mean?

She could never be sure. But she knew what she believed. There was no proof and never would be, but she wanted to believe it. Her heart believed.

He was like no other cat. Of that she was sure. He got immediately into her head and her heart. Came when she needed him. Actually protected her several times.

He'd found her in the coffin. And he'd led her to Blair. Lana remembered Blair's words. *"Nefra, leave me alone."*

What Lana — and Blair — believed was impossible. Wasn't it?

"I'm sorry, Nefra," she whispered to the cool, crisp morning as she started to school. "I'm sorry I couldn't return with you this time. But maybe, someday, I will know you again."

Terror is watching.

High on a hill,
trapped in the shadows,
something inside a dark house
is waiting...and watching.

THE HOUSE ON CHERRY STREET

**A three-book series
by Rodman Philbrick and Lynn Harnett**

Terror has a new home—and the children
are the only ones who sense it—from the
blasts of icy air in the driveway, to the windows
that shut like guillotines. Can Jason and Sally
stop the evil that lives in the dark?

**Book #1: THE HAUNTING
Book #2: THE HORROR
Book #3: THE FINAL NIGHTMARE**

NIGHTMARE HALL
where college is a
scream!

☐	BAR46014-5	#1 The Silent Scream	$3.50
☐	BAR47136-8	#2 The Roommate	$3.50
☐	BAR46015-3	#3 Deadly Attraction	$3.50
☐	BAR46013-7	#4 The Wish	$3.50
☐	BAR47137-6	#5 The Scream Team	$3.50
☐	BAR49452-X	#6 Guilty	$3.50
☐	BAR47690-4	#7 Pretty Please	$3.50
☐	BAR47703-X	#8 The Experiment	$3.50
☐	BAR47688-2	#9 The Night Walker	$3.50
☐	BAR47689-0	#10 Sorority Sister	$3.50
☐	BAR48133-9	#11 Last Date	$3.50
☐	BAR48154-1	#12 The Whisperer	$3.50
☐	BAR48321-8	#13 Monster	$3.50
☐	BAR48322-6	#14 The Initiation	$3.50
☐	BAR48353-6	#15 Truth or Die	$3.50
☐	BAR48358-7	#16 Book of Horrors	$3.50
☐	BAR48648-9	#17 Last Breath	$3.50
☐	BAR48649-7	#18 Win, Lose, or Die	$3.50

Available wherever you buy books, or use this order form.

- -

Scholastic Inc., P.O. Box 7502, 2931 East McCarty Street,
Jefferson City, MO 65102

Please send me the books I have checked above. I am enclosing $_____
(please add $2.00 to cover shipping and handling). Send check or money
order — no cash or C.O.D.s please.

Name _____ Age _____

Address _____

City _____ State/Zip _____

Please allow four to six weeks for delivery. Offer good in the U.S. only. Sorry, mail orders are not available to residents of Canada. Prices subject to change.   NH494

THRILLERS

D.E. Athkins
☐ MC45246-0 Mirror, Mirror $3.25
☐ MC45349-1 The Ripper $3.25
☐ MC44941-9 Sister Dearest $2.95

A. Bates
☐ MC45829-9 The Dead Game $3.25
☐ MC43291-5 Final Exam $3.25
☐ MC44582-0 Mother's Helper $3.50
☐ MC44238-4 Party Line $3.25

Caroline B. Cooney
☐ MC44316-X The Cheerleader $3.25
☐ MC41641-3 The Fire $3.25
☐ MC43806-9 The Fog $3.25
☐ MC45681-4 Freeze Tag $3.25
☐ MC45402-1 The Perfume $3.25
☐ MC44884-6 The Return of the Vampire $2.95
☐ MC41640-5 The Snow $3.25
☐ MC45680-6 The Stranger $3.50
☐ MC45682-2 The Vampire's Promise $3.50

Richie Tankersley Cusick
☐ MC43115-3 April Fools $3.25
☐ MC43203-6 The Lifeguard $3.25
☐ MC43114-5 Teacher's Pet $3.25
☐ MC44235-X Trick or Treat $3.25

Carol Ellis
☐ MC46411-6 Camp Fear $3.25
☐ MC44768-8 My Secret Admirer $3.25
☐ MC47101-5 Silent Witness $3.25
☐ MC46044-7 The Stepdaughter $3.25
☐ MC44916-8 The Window $2.95

Lael Littke
☐ MC44237-6 Prom Dress $3.25

Jane McFann
☐ MC46690-9 Be Mine $3.25

Christopher Pike
☐ MC43014-9 Slumber Party $3.50
☐ MC44256-2 Weekend $3.50

Edited by T. Pines
☐ MC45256-8 Thirteen $3.50

Sinclair Smith
☐ MC45063-8 The Waitress $2.95

Barbara Steiner
☐ MC46425-6 The Phantom $3.50

Robert Westall
☐ MC41693-6 Ghost Abbey $3.25
☐ MC43761-5 The Promise $3.25
☐ MC45176-6 Yaxley's Cat $3.25

Available wherever you buy books, or use this order form.
